UNDERSTANDING AFRICA

The Stories of Culture & Change

UNDERSTANDING AFRICA

The Stories of Culture & Change

A. H. M. Zehadul Karim
Nurazzura Mohamad Diah
Noor 'Azlan Mohd Noor
Norasikin Basir

PARTRIDGE

To order additional copies of this book, contact
Toll Free 800 101 2657 (Singapore)
Toll Free 1 800 81 7340 (Malaysia)
orders.singapore@partridgepublishing.com

www.partridgepublishing.com/singapore

CONTENTS

ACKNOWLEDGEMENT, PREFACE AND INTRODUCTION

This book on 'Understanding Africa' is a compilation of a number of articles explaining the analytical stories of culture-change in the African continent. A few articles of this book have been presented in draft form at an international conference held and organized by the Department of Sociology and Anthropology, International Islamic University Malaysia in December 2015. After the conference, the Department gave us the responsibility of editing this book on Africa, adding a few related articles from outside before this volume is published. We gratefully acknowledge the assistance and cooperation of our colleagues at the Department who have given us the responsibility of organizing this work and at same time, gaining their confidence and expectation that the final making of this work will be completed at the earliest. As an ongoing process, our present Head of Department, Dr. Rohaiza Rokis's special query on the manuscript inspires us to bring this challenging work into completion.

Africa is the world's second largest and second most populous continent presently containing approximately 1.1 billion people who live in an area of 30.3 million km. The harrowing historical legacy of Africa indicates that by the 1900s, much of its continent had been colonized by seven most powerful European nations, establishing their own colonial dominance and state systems to destroy African's own indigenous cultures and languages. At present, Africa consists of 54 sovereign countries, most of which have demarcations which were drawn during the European colonialism. There is much instability and ethnic marginalization in different parts of many countries in Africa, most of which had been exacerbated and was even created by the colonial rulers in the past. Walter Rodney (1982) in his book 'How Europe Underdeveloped Africa' clearly blamed Europe for subjecting this continent to the destructive force of its colonial masters. But it cannot be denied that Africa has always been in the past and also at present, a very resourceful continent with enormous storage of physical environment and ethno-cultural heritage. It is therefore essential to explore their way of life and cultural changes in different sectors, hence instigating us to compose a book covering the different issues related to this continent.

As indicated, this present book contains writings on diversified issues related to Africa and a good number of articles specifically focus on issues from the medical anthropological perspective. Accordingly, the first article of the book entitled "Knowledge, Attitude and Perception of Islamic Religious Leaders on Maternal Health Issues in Zamfara State, Northwest, Nigeria: A Qualitative Study" by Abdullahi Mohammed Maiwada *et al.*, is an evaluation of the roles and performances of a group of Islamic religious elites looking to improve the maternal health situation in a particular region of the country. It is also reflected in the title of the paper that Zamfara is one of the important states of Nigeria located in the northwestern region which has a total fertility rate of 7.5 and maternal mortality rate at 1049/100,000 live births, showing it is higher compared to the national average. It is therefore obvious that maternal health is quite significant in this context and accordingly, this issue is highlighted in this paper. The paper also covers the role of the Islamic religious leaders in this respect who are especially respected in this region; they are also very influential as key stakeholders in the decision-making process of the state. Since their views and opinions are well considered, the paper identifies a total of 64 leaders from both sexes who were interviewed most extensively to generate data for this paper. The paper concludes by showing the importance of these Islamic leaders who may be identified as effective partners in developing a sustainable system for maternal healthcare delivery system.

In telling the stories and pain of wife battering, Adam Andani and A.H.M. Zehadul Karim's article deals with a very sensitive issue relating to the social context of Ghana. Wife battering is a pandemic violence which is perpetrated by the male members of society and it is a sad condition faced by women in Ghana, which humiliates their socio-cultural status from the gender perspective. It is a serious crime allowing the gross violation of human rights which require special attention of researchers and policy planners as it endangers the life of the people in a societal context. The paper identifies a number of causes for wife battering in Ghana which seem to be interrelated but the factors of masculinity and male dominance the prime causes for this occurrence. Contextually, the paper has great significance in the field of social problems and as such the findings of such research can be generalized in wider perspectives of many developing societies as battery occurs everywhere in the world.

Healthcare service at present does not remain as the only responsibility of the government; rather, NGOs simultaneously play a significant role in dealing with this issue with the target of maintaining and preserving healthy lifestyles of the people. Contextually, Mahmudat O. Muhibbu-Din has written a very provocative article on NGOs and health services comparing the situation in Malaysia and Africa, thus highlighting the specific institutional contributions of the NGOs in both countries. In this perspective, the paper unravels the strengths and weaknesses of the NGOs and finally suggests ways as to how the healthcare services in general could be improved in the future.

Plenty of exciting issues on African countries and societies are published in newspapers in Malaysia which highlight the incidences occurring in different parts of the continent. Among many countries of Africa, Nigeria and Rwanda are portrayed as politically unstable where people are killing each other to gain and remain in power whereas Somalia has been depicted of having critical piracy problem at the seas. Apart from these broad issues, Malaysian newspapers also publish news relating to terrorism, sabotage created by the Boko Haram group, bomb attacks in a few regions and also the Ebola scare which reflect the variety of images of the region. Based on thematic content analysis of the news items published for a period of five months between May through July 2015, the article entitled "Representations of Africa and African Societies in a Malaysian Newspaper: An Analysis of The Star" specifically depended on The Star, a very influential newspaper in Malaysia. Nerawi Sedu and Nurazzura Mohamad Diah are the writers of this paper who indicate in their writing that most articles published in the newspaper reflect the African countries in a very negative way and it has been assumed that this type of negative portrayal will attract more readers to the paper, benefitting the owner from the commercial perspective. While many Third World countries can be presented with so many common features of fighting for power, high demographic pressure and illiteracy, the negative issues should be presented in such a way that they do not humiliate the people in that continent in the eyes of the global readers. From this perspective, the paper suggests some caution for journalism and this is the positive aspect of it.

S.M. Abdul Quddus and Sherrif Abu-Bakr Kaisi have written an article entitled 'Good Governance in the Health Sector of Malawi' focusing on the inequity in health status and showing its access to basic healthcare interventions in the country. Prior to their specific focus on Malawi's healthcare system, the paper describes its aspects in the context to Africa and Malaysia with subsequent comparisons being made. The paper adopts the model of good governance as suggested by UNDP to relate it to the healthcare system as an analytical framework for assessing the healthcare system in Malawi. It is based on an empirical research conducted on 120 patients and 15 service providers at the Queen Elizabeth Central Hospital who were interviewed most extensively to know about the healthcare quality and services in the institutional framework of the hospital. The paper identifies a number of factors that are responsible for constraining proper healthcare management in Malawi; the integrated remedies for such problems have also been suggested in the final part of the paper.

Adeela Rehman and Nurazzra Mohamad Diah in their paper on socio-cultural determinants in health discuss the wellbeing of the youth of Sub-Saharan Africa as they eventually affect the whole society. Sub-Saharan Africa is now the biggest region and recent impacts of globalization and modernization have affected all parts of it, allowing tremendous changes in every sphere of life. Due to demographic pressure and climate change, the region is now facing high rate of malnutrition; many people are infected by contagious diseases and the region is severely affected by poverty and unemployment. Due to such features, the youth in Sub-Saharan Africa have countenance with considerable impediment to get access to health services. Since most of the studies and research have focused on HIV/AIDS issue, the general well-being of the youth in terms of their nutritional status and health related issues are neglected. From this perspective, this research is academically fascinating and epistemologically relevant.

A.H.M Zehadul Karim
Nurazzura Mohamad Diah
Noor Azlan Mohd Noor
Norasikin Basir

x

NOTES ON CONTRIBUTORS

AHM Zehadul Karim has been teaching in universities for the last forty years and presently he is serving as a Professor at the Department of Sociology and Anthropology at the International Islamic University Malaysia (IIUM). He received his MA and PhD degrees in Anthropology from Syracuse University, USA. Dr. Karim also studied Sociology at the MA level at Lakehead University for one year in Canada; he also received his MA in Sociology from Dhaka University, Bangladesh. As of now, he has published and edited six books and has written 150 articles/papers which include published papers in professional international journals of the discipline, research reports and contributions to international conferences abroad.

Abdullahi Mohammed Maiwada is a Doctoral candidate at the Kulliyah of Allied Health Sciences of International Islamic University Malaysia, Kuantan Campus. A Public Health and Development Program Management Specialist, he has a Fellowship in International Public Health (FIPH) and Master of Public Health (MPH) from Tulane University, New Orleans, Louisiana, USA and Master of Social Science and Economics in Health Planning & Development from University Wales Swansea, UK. He has served variously as Senior Reproductive Health Program Manager and Senior Advisor with United States Agency for International Development (USAID/Nigeria); Northern Operations Manager of the Society for Family Health (SFH) and Consultant to Nigeria's National AIDS Control Agency (NACA), United Nations Development Program (UNDP) and Health Specialist at the World Bank, Nigeria Country Office. He has attended the Advanced Health Leadership Executive Course of the University of California, Berkeley and Bill & Melinda Gates Institute RH & Development Leadership Summer Institute of the John Hopkins School of Public Health, Baltimore, MD, USA. Maiwada also participated in the

Senior Executive Course of the National Institute for Policy and Strategic Studies (NIPSS), Kuru, Jos, Plateau State, Nigeria. He is a recipient of the Nigeria's National Honors of the Member of the Order of the Niger (MON). His research interest is reproductive and maternal health in Islam. He has published in several journals and made presentations at many national and international conferences.

Adam Andani Mohammed was the former President of African Student's Association Malaysia. A Ghanaian by nationality he received both his Master of Science and Ph.D. degrees in Sociology and Anthropology from the International Islamic University Malaysia (IIUM). His Bachelor of Arts degree is in Sociology with Political Science from University of Ghana, Legon. Adam took part in several international conferences as paper presenter and participant and has published in reputable journals. He was an Assistant Headmaster at Fathul-Mubeen Junior High School for two years and as a Headmaster for three years in Mahad-Tahiliyyah Islamic Junior High School both in Tamale, Ghana. In 2004, he worked at UNDP-African 2000 Network as a supervisor at Sagnarigu Women's Training Center Tamale. He has lectured and served on many conference and workshop programme committees. His research interests include women and children, social development, migration and refugees and social ecology. He participates in extra-curricular activities and volunteers for extra duties demonstrating an enthusiasm and true desire to be part of high institutional teams. He is currently a freelance researcher and has also proofread and edited a lot of manuscripts and theses.

Adeela Rehman is working as a lecturer at the Department of Gender Studies, Fatima Jinnah Women University, Pakistan. She did her Masters in Gender Studies (with distinction of silver medal) in 2007 from Fatima Jinnah Women University. She also completed her MS in Sociology in 2012 from the International Islamic University, Islamabad and is currently pursuing a PhD in Sociology & Anthropology, KIRKHS at the International Islamic University Malaysia (IIUM). Her research areas are medical/health sociology, culture and gender issues on which she has presented at a number of national and international conferences and seminars as presenter and as guest speaker. Being a homeopathic physician, gender expert and a medical sociologist, she is interested to study women's health issues and problems with reference to healthcare system of Pakistan. She has also received a number of awards for her professional activities and always volunteers for various academic and non-academic activities. She also visited The University of Texas, Austin USA as a visiting faculty in 2013. In recognition of her teaching excellence she was awarded with "Rosina C. Chia Teaching of Excellence Award 2015" presented by Global Partners in Education USA on 12th of May 2015 at Global Partner's Education Conference in China. A numbers of publication in indexed journals are also credited to her.

Mahmudat O. Muhibbu-Din is currently a lecturer at University of Maiduguri, Borno State, Nigeria. A former lecturer at Fountain University, Oshogbo, she works as an active member in various capacities in administration and management of the University. She is also an awardee of the 2010 South-South Programme, Council for Development of Social Science Research in Africa (CODESRIA). She writes on American gegemony, financial crisis and the rise of China. She has published studies on gender, Islamic feminism and development, Nigerian politics and government and has just completed her doctoral research on NGOs and human security in Nigeria. Mahmudat has attended conferences locally and internationally and presented paper on different topics relating to governance and politics.

Nerawi Sedu is currently a lecturer at the Department of Communication, Kulliyyah of Islamic Revealed Knowledge and Human Sciences (KIRKHS), International Islamic University Malaysia (IIUM). He obtained his Doctor of Philosophy from the School of Journalism, University of Queensland Australia. He has been with this department for more than ten years. He teaches courses on media system and contemporary issues in communication, media law and ethics and intercultural communication. His areas of interests are media studies and journalism. Nerawi has written a number of articles based on his content analyses of newspapers. He has also presented research-based papers at a number of international conferences in Malaysia as well as abroad.

Nik Mazlan Mamat graduated with a Bachelor in Dietetics and started a career as a dietitian with Universiti Kebangsaan Malaysia. He obtained his Masters of Science from London School of Hygiene and Tropical Medicine; and later Doctor of Philosophy from University of Aberdeen, Scotland. He joined the International Islamic University Malaysia in 2004, to serve at the Kulliyyah of Allied Health Sciences, Kuantan Campus. In 2008, he was appointed as the Dean for the Kulliyyah of Allied Health Sciences until May 2014. He now serves as Deputy Campus Director of IIUM Kuantan Campus. As an academician, his research interests include appetite regulation, eating behaviour and obesity and he has contributed academic articles and chapters for academic books in the area. At the national level, he sits in several committees in the Ministry of Health, including as a member of the National Coordinating Committee for Food and Nutrition (NCCFN). Nik Mazlan chaired the first Committee on Standards for Health and Medical Sciences, and serves as a Panel Assessor for the Malaysian Qualification Agency (MQA).

Nor Azlina A. Rahman is currently an Assistant Professor at the Department of Biomedical Science of Kulliyyah of Allied Health Sciences, International Islamic University Malaysia (IIUM). Previously a medical officer at the Ministry of Health Malaysia after getting her Medical Bachelor and Bachelor of Surgery (MBBS) from Universiti Malaya in 1996, she started teaching public health related subjects such as Epidemiology, Research Methodology, Biostatistics and a few others for undergraduate and post-graduate students in IIUM after obtaining her Master of Community Medicine specializing in Epidemiology and Biostatistics from Universiti Sains Malaysia in 2007. She was also appointed a member of International Islamic University Malaysia Ethics Committee (IREC) since the end of 2014 until now and has been reviewing a lot of researches done in IIUM for ethical approval. Although her interest is in non-communicable diseases such as diabetes mellitus, she had also been invited to co-supervise a number of post-graduate students and co-research a few studies in various fields relating to community medicine.

Nurazzura Mohamad Diah is an Associate Professor at the Department of Sociology & Anthropology, KIRKHS, International Islamic University Malaysia (IIUM). She joined the department in 1997. She was the department's chair from 2011-2016. Nurazzura obtained a PhD in Anthropology from the University of Western Australia, Perth in 2010. She specializes in women's health. Her research interests include aboriginal health, body image, women's well-being, middle-aged crisis, health tourism and sport's health. She has published a number of work on health-related issues including menopause, pap smear and media coverage on health issues. She is the life member of the Malaysian Menopause Society (MMS) and Qualitative Reasearch Association Malaysia (QRAM). She supervises postgraduate research on healthcare services, disability, aborigines' participation in sports and body image. Currently, her research focuses on the socio-cultural determinants of parental refusal on vaccination and Zika coverage in the media.

SM Abdul Quddus is an Associate Professor of Public Policy and Governance at the Department of Political Science and is the Deputy Director of IIUM Centre for Strategic Continuing Education and Training (IIUM CRESCENT) at the International Islamic University Malaysia. He earned his Bachelor of Social Science (Hons.) and Master of Social Science degrees in Public Administration from the Chittagong University (Bangladesh), and MPhil and Ph.D. in Public Administration from the University of Bergen (Norway). He has been lecturing at different universities (in Bangladesh, Norway, and Malaysia) for 23 years. He is an executive committee member of Policy Research Centre (UK); life member of the Malaysian Social Science Association (MSSA) and a member (2017-2018) of the International Political Science Association (IPSA). He specializes in the study of professions; globalization and governance; democracy, civil society and inclusive development; and politics, administration and organization in the Muslim world. He has authored and edited four books/monographs and contributed over two dozens of articles/book chapters in internationally refereed journals/books published in the US, Norway, Malaysia and other parts of the world. He is the recipient of Guest Scholar Fellowship (2001) awarded by the Nordic Institute of Asian Studies, Copenhagen, Denmark.

Sherrif Abu-Bakr Kaisi is a senior lecturer and Dean of Academics/Dean Faculty of Development and Applied Sciences at Skyway University (SU) in Malawi. He earned his Bachelor of Arts in Arabic Language and Public Administration (Tripoli, Libya) and Master of Human Science degree in Political Science from the International Islamic University Malaysia (IIUM). He has been lecturing at different private universities in Malawi for 4 and half years. He is the publicity secretary of the Islamic commission for justice and freedom ICJF (MALAWI); an executive member of Skyway University Research Team (SURT); and an upcoming member of Political Science Association of Malawi (PSAM). He is specialized in the following areas: good governance, decentralization, democracy, civil society organizations, sustainable development, community development; conflict resolution and peace building; African politics, development in Sub-Sahara Africa. He has attended various international conferences such as Economic Analysis and Planning for Cities and Towns of Africa, Fujian Province, CHINA2015. He is a columnist in the Globe Newspaper (MALAWI) covering topics ranging from politics, good governance, religion and issues concerning socio-economic and sustainable development.

Suzanah Abdul Rahman obtained her BSc (Hons) in Biomedical Sciences and PhD degrees from the University of Bradford, United Kingdom. Upon completion of her PhD, she returned to Malaysia and took up a lecturer position at the Kuantan Campus of the International Islamic University Malaysia (IIUM). Courses taught include toxicology, research methodology and ethics, environmental health and ocular pharmacology. Suzanah is the pioneer academic for the Kulliyyah/Faculty of Allied Health Sciences in IIUM and she has been the Deputy Dean since 2003, heading various Deputy Dean offices for Academic Affairs, Research & Postgraduate and also Student Affairs including as the Deputy Director for the Institutional & Academic Quality Management Office of IIUM Kuantan. Her skills include that in leadership and quality management as she has undergone numerous training such as by Dale Carnegie & Associates, Inc. and SIRIM. She is a qualified ISO Internal Auditor in IIUM and has contributed to the Malaysian Qualifications Agency (MQA) as a Programme and Self-Accreditation Panel Assessor and Auditor since 2010. Suzanah is also an appointed member since 2011, of the IIUM Research Ethics Committee

(IREC). For her work in reproductive toxicology, Suzanah has received various fundings namely from the Ministry of Higher Education (ERGS) and the Ministry of Agriculture and Agro-Based Industry (NRGS). Her research specialization includes the use of Natural Products in Assisted Reproductive Techniques (ART) and the application of toxicology in the determination of adverse health reactions. Suzanah has since conducted related workshops in embryology at university level and has received awards for the presentation and exhibition of her work in paternal drug toxicity and natural product effects on gametes of especially mouse and embryo.

Tukur. A. Muhammad-Baba has been Director, Centre for Peace Studies and, concurrently, Head, Department of Sociology, Usmanu Danfodiyo University, Sokoto. He has a B.Sc. Sociology from Ahmadu Bello University, 1978, MA in Development Studies from University of East Anglia, Norwich, UK and PhD Sociology from the University of Missouri-Columbia (1987). His other experiences include Director of Academic Planning at the Federal University of Technology, Yola (1992-1993); Consultant Sociologist/Survey Logistics Coordinator, Health Care Financing, Costs and Utilization Study, Sokoto Health Project, 1988–1989, Co-Researcher on a joint study of Pastoral Fulani transhumance in the North West for the National Livestock Projects Unit (1990-1992), General Manager, Nigerian Security Printing and Minting Company; Visiting Scholar at the Institute of Conflict Analysis and Resolution (ICAR), George Mason University (Winter Semester, 2009). His areas of research/scholarly interests include social change and development, economy and society, social conflict, protest movements, social policy, state and society in the Sokoto Caliphate and historiography, among others. He has a number of publications and research papers to his credit.

KNOWLEDGE, ATTITUDE AND PERCEPTION OF ISLAMIC RELIGIOUS LEADERS ON MATERNAL HEALTH ISSUES IN ZAMFARA STATE, NORTHWEST, NIGERIA: A QUALITATIVE STUDY

Abdullahi Mohammed Maiwada, Nik Mazlan
Mamat, Suzanah Abd. Rahman,
Nor Azlina A. Rahman & Tukur Baba

INTRODUCTION

According to the Nigeria Demographic and Health Survey (DHS) 2013, maternal mortality is an aspect of adult mortality that is of particular interest in the Nigerian context. Worldwide, the 10 countries with the highest maternal mortality ratios are in Africa, and an estimated 14% of maternal deaths globally occur in Nigeria (United Nations Economic Commission for Africa [UNECA], 2013). Data from Nigeria's Five-Year Countdown Strategy for achieving Millennium Development Goals (MDGs) show that maternal mortality fell from 800 deaths per 100,000 live births in 2003 (FMOH, 2005) to 545 deaths per 100,000 live births in 2008. Progress related to this goal has been slow and challenges remain (National Population Commission, 2009). In addition to other interventions designed to reduce maternal mortality and achieve the MDGs' target of 250 deaths per 100,000 live births in Nigeria, the government, in collaboration with development partners, has continued to improve access to quality maternal health services through the Community Health Insurance Scheme and the Midwives Service Scheme (Federal Ministry of Health, 2007; FMOH, 2009). Maternal mortality is an important indicator for women's programmes and reproductive health programmes in the country (Federal Ministry of Health, 2010).

A maternal death is defined as any death reported during pregnancy, childbirth, or within two months after the birth or termination of a pregnancy. In the World Bank 2008 Report on the *State of the World's Mothers*, Nigeria ranked 70 out of 71 less-developed countries, as one of the worst places in the world to be a mother (WHO, 2010). The maternal mortality rate (MMR) in 2005 was estimated at 1,100/100,000 live births in a WHO, UNICEF, UNFPA and World Bank analysis report of 2008 and it is considered to be even higher in the northern States, particularly the North East with MMR of 1549/100,000 live birth (WHO 2008). However, the 2008 DHS indicated that some progress has been made in reducing maternal mortality. Thus, it estimated the MMR for Nigeria to be 545 deaths per 100,000 live births. Also, according to the NHDS (2008), 47% of Nigerian women had 4 or more antenatal visits and 58% received antenatal care from a skilled provider. The 2008 survey showed only 39% were attended to at delivery by a skilled provider, about one third of births or 35% occurred in health facilities while 62% occured at home (National Population Commission, 2008).

Zamfara State is one of the states in Northern Nigeria, located in the northwest geopolitical zone. It has a population of about 3.4 million people. According to CBN report of 2006, the state has a poverty rate of about 75-80% and is one of the educationally less advantaged states in Nigeria. Zamfara State has a total fertility rate of 7.5 and maternal mortality rate of 1049/100,000 live births (Doctor et al, 2012) as compared to the national average of 545/100,000 live births (MOH Zamfara State, 2008). The current use of any modern family planning method in Zamfara (among married women aged 15-49) is 2% while the percentage of women who gave birth in the last 5 years who received antenatal care from a skilled provider is only 18% and those with a skilled attendant at delivery stood at 8% (National Population Commission, 2008). These statistics are among the worst in the country. Since the institution of the Shariah Islamic legal system in Zamfara State, a number of Islamic institutions

2

and organizations are discharging some duties and responsibilities for enshrining and ensuring the Islamic legal system is adhered to and followed. They include the Shariah Research Council, Islamic Preaching Board, Hisbah (Islamic police), Zakat and Endowment Board as well as the Ministry for Religious affairs.

The Islamic religious leaders are therefore respected and command a big followership in state affairs; they are influential and key stakeholders in decision making in the states' and even individual affairs. Consequently, their views and opinion are always sought for by the followership in decision to seek for care and accept maternal health. In that regards, the Islamic religious leaders occupy an important position in Muslim communities especially in Zamfara State and northern Nigerian states. They thus influence the lives of their subjects and societal development in general through preaching and their actions. Members of their communities and followership look up to them on issues of family life, societal norms, justice, education, commerce and health. They wield so much unwritten influence among their followers. Studies concerning Islamic religious leaders are not common and therefore few literature on them is available (Underwood, 2000). They are interpreters of the Islamic legal system - the Shariah, jurisprudence and ways of life - thus an important segment to examine and review their knowledge, attitude and perception of maternal health issues and even deaths.

The IIUM/HPP project is a pilot intervention project that was implemented between 2013 and 2014 in some selected communities in Gusau Local Government area of Zamfara State. IIUM/HPP research intervention project is supported partly by the Kulliyah of Allied Health of the International Islamic University Malaysia through a mini grant. The project focused on addressing the barriers to Maternal and Newborn Health (MNH), working in the intervention communities by conducting health promotion and community mobilization activities to contribute to improvement in maternal health and reduction of maternal deaths in Zamfara State. The project was assisted by community volunteers and Islamic religious leaders to create awareness on maternal mortality and maternal health in some selected communities. During the period of the project implementation, community members were sensitized and mobilized to support women, especially those pregnant to attend antenatal care clinics (ANC) and encourage hospital delivery during child birth. Some of the community mobilization activities include health education activities, dramas, health talks and presentations of sermon (*khutbah*) by Islamic religious leaders during Muslim congregations. The project also adopted and adapted some existing and past projects' information, education and communication materials such as educational leaflets to enlighten the community members on maternal health and dangers leading to maternal deaths.

MATERIALS AND METHODS
Study Area

Zamfara State is located in the northwestern part of Nigeria at latitude 120°N and longitude 60°E with an altitude of 420m. Zamfara was carved out of the former Sokoto State on 1st October, 1996. It occupies a land area of about 38,418 square kilometres. It is bounded in the North by Sokoto State and the Republic of Niger, in the west by Kebbi and Niger States, in the east by Katsina State and Kaduna State in the south.

Methodology

A total of 64 Islamic religious leaders were interviewed; 44 males and 20 females were interviewed using open ended questions and an interview guide. Also six focus group discussions (FGDs) were also conducted for three male and three female groups. All interviews were conducted in the local language of Hausa which is the commonly spoken language in the area. The interviews were tape recorded and notes taken during both the in-depth interviews and FGDs.

The Zamfara State Health Research and Ethics committee's approval was obtained as was the approval of the IIUM Research and ethics committee before the conduct of the research intervention project. At all levels, permission of the relevant agencies and gatekeepers were sought while all the respondents gave their verbal informed consent before any of the interviews.

Inclusion criteria: Islamic preachers, Islamic scholars, Islamiyyah teachers, leaders and administrators of Islamic organizations in the State. The Islamic religious leaders also included both female Islamic scholars and their male counterparts.

Exclusion criteria: Those who did not have enough knowledge on Islamic education and non-Muslims were excluded from this study.

RESULTS

1) Knowledge of the Islamic Religious Leaders on Maternal Health Issues

The Islamic religious leaders' knowledge and understanding of maternal health issues was high, especially on maternal health issues from the Islamic perspective and viewpoint. All the Islamic religious leaders knew one or more women who had lost their lives during childbirth or as a result of pregnancy. Some of them mentioned having to conduct the funeral prayer of some of the women who lost their lives during pregnancy or while giving birth. The religious leaders observed that it was pathetic and something that is of concern not only to donor partners but to state governments and other stakeholders.

The religious leaders were of the opinion that much needs to be done to avert and reduce these deaths and morbidities among women. As such, they all see themselves as having a role to play, especially in enlightening and informing the public of maternal death situations in their localities. One of the respondents has this to say, *"maternal health is encompassed in the Islamic injunctions as part of the role of the husband to ensure that his wife is healthy during pregnancy"*.

In a similar vein, another renowned scholar in the state expressed concern on the rate which women die as a result of pregnancy, *"I am concerned at the rate we have so many women dying due to giving birth either at the hospital or at home"*. All of the Islamic religious leaders, when asked about issues of maternal health, answered in the affirmative that they are aware of it, whether at personal or institutional levels.

A group of the Islamic religious leaders in an FGD said, *"we formed an association to fight the poor maternal death indices and to advocate for changes among our people and government"*. In a related development, two of the Islamic religious leaders separately mentioned approaching the state government to do something to improve the maternal health situation in the state. As one of the scholars said, *"I personally booked an appointment with the Commissioner of Health to discuss this matter, of (which) I am quite aware of it"*.

On their knowledge of any state policy to improve the maternal health situation in Zamfara State, all of the Islamic religious leaders said they do not know of any and if there is none *"then the state government needs to put one in place"* according to one of the respondents.

The religious leaders opined that its part of their duties as leaders to help avert deaths and suffering among the people, especially maternal deaths and it is within their jurisdiction to educate others, especially husbands, in-laws and government office holders to live up to their responsibilities in managing family, communal and general public affairs. When asked on early marriage, the Islamic scholars were less disposed to delayed marriage but expressed awareness on the likely dangers it may result to such as Vesicovaginal Fistula (VVF) and even death of the girl or woman.

2) *Attitude of the Islamic Religious Leaders on Maternal Health Issues*

The Islamic religious leaders saw it as a form of *"Jihad"* to inform their followers and educate them on maternal and newborn health thereby contributing to reduction of maternal deaths. According to one of the Islamic religious leaders, *"He who saves one believer's life saves the whole community"* and he who saves the *"Ummah will be abundantly rewarded by Allah in the hereafter".*

All the Islamic religious leaders interviewed observed that it is part of their religious duties to enlighten the followers on the dangers leading to maternal deaths and support programmes and activities that will improve maternal health *"in our communities and areas".* All the respondents were said to have preached or given sermon on the need for husbands, parents and in-laws to allow their wives or wards to attend antenatal care or even deliver at the hospital in order to avoid complications or deaths of the mother during childbirth.

One of the respondents in an in-depth interview mentioned that it is surprising that *"it's only in the Muslim dominated communities of northern Nigeria that we have high maternal mortality, why".* The respondents therefore opined that they owe it a duty and onerous task for Islamic religious leaders to stop the deaths of women during childbirth or as a result of pregnancy. That pregnancy and childbirth should be a period of joy, not of sorrow for the woman, husband and family members.

Some of the Islamic religious leaders mentioned allowing their wives, daughters, sisters or daughters-in-law to attend antenatal care visits during pregnancy. One of the prominent scholars said, "*I personally took my wife and daughter to the clinic for ANC, as I know its importance*". In the discussions, the Islamic religious leaders expressed shock and disappointment on how pregnant women are sometimes poorly treated by their husbands or family members; they all called on the men and stakeholders to take care of women in general and those pregnant in particular. The Islamic religious leaders mentioned that the Qur'an and Sunnah of Prophet Muhammad (SAW) enjoin Muslims to be kind to women as contained in Surah 2, Verse 228 of the Qur'an. In their assertion some of the respondents cited examples that the *fuqaha* (learned Islamic jurists) said the sustenance and care of a pregnant woman is compulsory upon the husband even at divorce as prescribed in the Holy Qur'an, Surah 65, Verse 6 "*…if they are pregnant continue to care for them until they deliver and when they give birth to child compensate them for breast feeding their child and even after…*".

3) Perceptions of the Islamic Religious Leaders on Maternal Health Issues

The Islamic religious leaders viewed issues of maternal health as matters of importance which concern family life and consequently affect the *ummah*. Mostly they are all positive in their responses to the perception of MNH.

An Islamic religious leader had this to say on discussing or talking about maternal health "*I have confidence in preaching the MNCH issues*". Also an Islamic religious leader in an in-depth interview said he encourages women to attend antenatal care and he allows his wives and family members to visit the clinic for ANC, "*I practice what I preach*". Initially, many scholars did not talk about MNCH, but now we preach openly and in this community almost all women attend ANC, hospital delivery and immunization. The Islamic religious leaders perceived that the issues of maternal health should be "*a concern for all*" as said by one of them. They all mentioned that Islam is not oblivious to "*the hardship that the woman goes through carrying the pregnancy for nine months and breastfeeding the child for about eighteen months until the child is weaned as is indicated in one verse of the Qur'an, Surah 31, Verse 14 and Surah 46, Verse 15*". The Islamic religious leaders said, *"all Muslims and non-Muslims alike are enjoined to show sympathy to the parents especially the mother who suffered to carry the pregnancy of a child"*. In one of the FGDs, all the Islamic religious leaders indicated knowing of a case of maternal death, complications during birth or illnesses. The Islamic religious leaders mentioned some of the ways maternal health can be improved and the roles they can all play. They said, *"we all have roles to play as prescribed in the Qur'an and Hadith"*, and *"we are vicegerents to the teachings of Prophet Muhammad (SAW)"*. One female Islamic scholar gave an example as to why pregnant women need to be cared for according to Fuqha-Islamic jurist saying *"good thinking comes from a healthy body"* as contained in Tafsir of Al-Mughirah and therefore the need to have both healthy pregnant and non-pregnant women. In general, the perception of the Islamic religious leaders on maternal health issues and maternal deaths is indicative of their understanding and the role they can play in reducing maternal deaths in low resource countries like Northern Nigeria.

SUGGESTIONS AND RECOMMENDATIONS BY THE ISLAMIC RELIGIOUS LEADERS

The project should involve Islamic organizations and institutions in these similar activities in Zamfara State, Northern Nigeria and the country at large. Educational institutions and universities like the Islamic University Katsina, and the Usmanu Danfodiyo University, Sokoto should emulate the activities of IIUM/HPP projects. Governments at federal, state and local levels including international and bilateral organizations should provide funding for similar programmes in Northern Nigeria, targeting communities through the Islamic religious leaders both males and females.

Projects such as these should continue to advocate for maternal health projects through Islamic organizations, associations, and movements such as Jamaatul Nasril Islam (JNI), Jamaatul Izalatul Bid'ah Wa Ikamatus Sunnah (JIBWIS), Nasrullahil Fathi (NASFAT), etc. to create awareness to reduce the rate at which Muslim women are lost during childbirth or delivery in order to stay true to the saying of Prophet Muhammad (SAW) *"marry and give birth to children so that I will be proud of you"*. The religious leaders were of the opinion that programmers should use Islamic teachings, tenets and principles in programme design, planning and implementation as *"there is nothing left unknown in Islam"*. Islam is an up-to date and informed religion.

DISCUSSION

Based on the thinking among scholars and programmers on the perception of the Islamic religious leaders on maternal health issues and maternal deaths, their responses are positive and welcomed as they perceived that there is the need for all hands to be on deck to stop or avert the alarming high rates of maternal deaths in Northern Nigeria. As socio-cultural and religious barriers are some of the factors that limit utilization and uptake of maternal health services in predominantly Muslim north (Butuwa et al., 2010). The Islamic religious leaders expressed readiness to support and create more awareness on the matter and to further the discussions during their da'awah and Islamic propagation activities.

There is a significant paradigm shift and change in the attitude of the Islamic religious leaders when compared to some years back, where they did not even discuss issues such as this as they saw it as "a Western agenda" which they viewed as having some hidden intention. The study also shows how the Islamic religious leaders view the issues of women's health and gender issues.

The Islamic religious leaders are highly respected and command a big followership in state affairs; they are influential and key stakeholders in decision making in the states' and even individual affairs (Mairiga et al., 2007). Consequently, their views and opinion are always sought after by the followership in decisions to seek for care and accept maternal health. In that regard, the Islamic religious leaders occupy an important position in Muslim communities, especially in Zamfara State and Northern Nigerian States. They thus influence the lives of their subjects and societal development in general through preaching and their actions. Members of their communities and followership look up to them on issues of family life, societal norms, justice, education, commerce and health. They wield so much unwritten influence among their followers.

Faith based groups play a significant role in maternal health providing critical outreach in the communities they serve (Chand & Patterson, 2007). Islam as a complete way of life thus confirms and legitimizes the social role of Islamic scholars. The Islamic religious leaders can determine the success or failure of development programmes regardless of the efforts put in by the constituted authorities or as designed by the donors, partners or NGOs. The huge effect that Islamic scholars have had on the rejection and temporary halting of immunization as well as its acceptance in some states in Northern Nigeria is a good example (Underwood, 2000). In rural and marginalised areas where literacy is low and access to mass media is limited, religious leaders are often one of the few reliable and effective communication channels, endowed with a powerful platform for shedding misperceptions and promoting positive behaviours, including men's roles in improving women's ability to seek healthcare. Islamic religious leaders (*ulama*) are important in influencing societal norms, values and behaviours in societies where there is high illiteracy and the outlook is conservative.

In Zamfara State and Northern Nigeria and other parts of the world, Islamic religious leaders are respected and in some cases revered and thus command a lot of respect. Therefore, understanding how they perceive MNH issues, their understanding and attitude to maternal health will consequently reduce socio-cultural barriers to uptake of maternal health services and reduction of maternal deaths. In addition, understanding the roles of Islamic religious leaders and their social obligation in propagating information on MNH services utilization, ANC visits and hospital delivery is critical success of any programme that will aim at contributing to the reduction of maternal deaths. The Islamic religious leaders are therefore important mediums for information, education and communication (IEC) in improving maternal health services uptake. Thus, the Islamic religious leaders are "health educators/promoters" in their own right on issues of maternal health. Programmers, implementing agencies and donor partners therefore need to collaborate and work with the Islamic religious leaders in achieving the set targets of maternal mortality reduction and improving uptake of maternal health services, especially in the northern part of Nigeria if the gloomy picture of maternal deaths is to be reduced.

As discussed by Chand and Patterson (2007), this study further reinforces the fact that besides being a religious authority, the Islamic religious leaders also command a strong foothold in their respective communities; they play a critical role in shaping their community's beliefs and attitudes on a range of aspects of their lives including maternal health and other health related issues. The Islamic religious leaders are expected to uphold the normative traditions of an Islamic society and act as gatekeepers for their achievement. These characteristics make the Islamic religious leaders communication mediums who can be used to propagate and increase acceptance of maternal health programmes through the Islamic perspectives. It is in this regard that a comprehensive intervention involving the Islamic religious leaders approach was implemented in some selected communities of Zamfara State, northwest Nigeria in promoting maternal health. The need to involve key and critical stakeholders such as the Islamic religious leaders need not to be overemphasized as suggested in a study by Kawuwa et al. (2007).

CONCLUSION

The knowledge, attitude and perception of Islamic religious leaders to maternal health issues and maternal deaths in Northern Nigeria is a poser for using them as change agents and promoters of maternal health across the state in order to reduce the socio-cultural barriers to maternal health uptake and reduce maternal mortality. This study is therefore dispelling the myth and misconception about the negative attitude and perception of Islamic religious leaders. The study also suggests that they are knowledgeable of the menace of maternal morbidity and mortality in their localities. They are also a reference point of their followers, whom if engaged during the design and implementation of MNH program will serve as referral agents for the uptake of MNH in Northern Nigeria.

The involvement of Islamic religious leaders in maternal health intervention programmes has a positive influence on the knowledge and utilization of MNCH services among community members with the Islamic religious leaders serving as role models and health promoters or communicators. The Islamic religious leaders viewed the IIUM/HPP pilot project as a good and welcoming development coming from an international university with religious affiliation to Islam; it is *"therefore welcomed"*. It is thus recommended that organizations such Islamic Development Bank (IsDB), and Organization for Islamic Countries (OIC) should come up with programmes that target and address MNH issues among Muslims and non-Muslims and their communities such as the pilot research project supported by IIUM in order to promote what was achieved by the project within a short period of time. There are several calls for up scaling this project and its replication in similar settings by the religious leaders and other stakeholders interviewed. The Islamic religious leaders who served in various capacities to their community members can help reduce or remove the barriers to seeking care and utilization by giving *fatwas* on whether a woman in labour has to wait for her husband's or in-laws' permission to seek care or not. The Islamic religious leaders can pass and share information in various ways and forms through Khutbah- during Friday congregations, at schools and Islamiyyah, *tafsir*- which is daily and weekly preaching, naming and wedding fatiha and ceremonies. The Islamic religious leaders and faith based leaders can be effective partners in developing sustainable system for maternal healthcare delivery in low resource countries.

REFERENCES

Doctor, H.V, Olatunji, A, Findley, S E, Afenyadu, GY, Abdulwahab, A, Jumare, A. Maternal mortality in northern Nigeria: findings of a health and demographic surveillance system in Zamfara State, Nigeria Tropical Doctor 2012:1-4 Doi:10.1258/td.2012.120062:

Doctor, H.V, Findley, S E, Afenyadu, GY. Estimating Maternal Mortality Level in rural Northern Nigeria by Sisterhood Method, International Journal of Population Research August 2012, doi:10.1155/2012/464657

WHO, UNICEF, UNFPA and The World Bank (2005): Maternal Mortality estimates in 2005.

WHO, UNICEF, UNFPA and The World Bank (2010): Trend in Maternal Mortality 1990 to 2008 Federal Ministry of Health (Nigeria): National Strategic Health Development Plan (NSHDP), 2010.

Federal Ministry of Health (Nigeria): The Nigeria National Health Policy, 2004.

National Population Commission. Nigeria Demographic and Health Survey 2003. Abuja, Calverton MD: NPC, ORC Macro, 2004.

National Population Commission, ICF Macro. Nigeria Demographic and Health Survey, 2008. Abuja: NPC and ICF Macro, 2009.

Federal Ministry of Health (Nigeria): The IMNCH Strategy, 2009.

WHO, UNICEF, UNFPA and The World: Trends in Maternal Mortality: 1990 to 2008 Bank, 2010.

Federal Ministry of Health (Nigeria): Assessment of implementation of the 2001-2006 National Reproductive Health Policy and Strategic Framework and Plan, (2007).

Federal Ministry of Health (Nigeria) and World Health Organization (WHO), Road Map for Accelerating the Attainment of the MDGs related to Maternal and Newborn Health in Nigeria (2005).

Zamfara State Ministry of Health (2009), Report of Proceedings of the First Zamfara State Council on Health, June 2008.

Doctor HV, Bairagi R, Findley SE, Helleringer S, Tukur D. Northern Nigeria Maternal, Newborn and Child Health Programme: selected analyses from population-based baseline survey. Open Demography J 2011; 4:11–21.

Doctor HV, Findley SE, Jumare A. Evidence-based health programme planning in northern Nigeria: results from the Nahuche Health and Demographic Surveillance System Pilot Census. J Rural Trop Public Hlth 2011; 10:21–8.

National Population Commission, ICF Macro. Nigeria Demographic and Health Survey, 2008. Abuja: NPC and ICF Macro, 2009.

Mairiga AG, Kyari O, Kullima A, Abdullahi H. (2007). Knowledge, Perception and Attitude of Islamic Scholars towards Reproductive Health Programs in Borno State, Nigeria. Afr. J Rep Hlth; 11:98-106.

Butuwa NN, Tukur B, Idris H, Adiri H, Taylor KD. (2010). Knowledge and Perception of Maternal Health in Kaduna State, Northern Nigeria. Afr. J Rep Hlth, (Sp.Iss); 14(3):71-76.

Underwood C. Islamic Precepts and family planning: The Perception of Jordanian Religious Leaders and Their Constituents. Intl Fam Planning Persp, 2000, 26(3):110-117.

Chand S and Patterson J. Faith based model for improving maternal and new born health. USAID, Sept. 2007.

Kawuwa M B, Mairiga A G, Usman H A. Community perspective of maternal mortality: Experience from Konduga local government area, Borno state, Nigeria. Ann Afr Med 2007; 6:109-14.

2

TELLING STORIES OF PAIN: EXPERIENCE OF WIFE BATTERY IN GHANA AND MALAYSIA

Adam Andani Mohammed & AHM Zehadul Karim

INTRODUCTION

Domestic violence is one of the widespread global phenomena affecting societies. Many terms like "domestic violence", "domestic abuse" (Dobash & Dobash, 1984) and "woman abuse" (Mullender & Morley, 2001) are used frequently in the UK and in Europe (Borg, 2003) while "family violence" and "intimate partner violence" are used more in the USA (Barnett et al., 2005; Loseke et al., 2005), "spousal abuse", "woman abuse", "wife abuse" and others are often interchangeably used to describe violence perpetrated by men against women. This phenomenon is condoned in various ways by society since time immemorial as it occurs in many settings and in many hands, including those of relatives, couples, acquaintances, employers and the state (Watts & Zimmerman, 2002; Kishor & Johnson 2004; WHO, 2006; Hossain et al., 2014; Gupta et al., 2013; Paula, 2010; Adjiwanour & LeGrand, 2014; Adu-gyamfi, 2014; Pool et al., 2014; Susan, 2013; Ng et al., 2011). In this context, a problem of pandemic proportions includes physical and sexual attacks against women in the home, in the family or in an intimate relationship. Studies have shown that in reality these relationships are not always peaceful and secure (Merkin, 2013; Jewkes & Morrell, 2010; Crissman, Adanu & Harlow, 2012; Dutton, 2006; Adu-gyamfi, 2014; Meekers et al., 2013 Lawson, 2003; Ng et al.,

2011). The victims are at high risk of experiencing psychological and emotional problems like depression, suicide, anxiety, substance abuse or post-traumatic stress disorder which sometimes require medical attention (WHO, 2006; Diop-Sidibe et al., 2006; Verelst et al., 2014; Susan 2013; Binahayati, 2011; Malta et al., 2012; Gilchrist et al., 2010).

Studies show that it is a family and social issue affecting the socioeconomy, health, cultural life and emotions of people across the world and thus need attention (Rezaeian, 2010; Valentine et al., 2011; Finnbogadottir et al., 2014; Jacob, 2011). As such the United Nations' General Assembly promoted the International Decade for Women (1975-1985) which paved the way for gender activists to advocate for change in violence against women. The advocates gained the recognition of women's rights as human rights at the United Nations Conference on Human Rights held in Vienna, Austria 1993. The International Conference on Population and Development in Cairo in 1994, the World Summit for Social Development in Copenhagen in 1995, the Fourth World Conference on Women in Beijing in 1995 in China and the United Nations' Conference on Human Settlement in 1996 were other platforms on which this issue received global concern and recognition (Salazar, 2014; Adu-gyamfi, 2014; Tumwesigye et al., 2012). These conferences declared wife battery as a violation of women's rights during the Beijing Declaration and Platform for Action, an issue of global importance (Kishor & Johnson, 2004; Adu-gyamfi, 2014; Meekers et al., 2013; Adebayo, 2014; Susan, 2013; Archampong, 2010).

Despite the international concern over violence as a crime against humanity, women in most societies across the globe, including in Ghana and Malaysia, are still subjected to various kinds of violence perpetrated by their husbands. The traditional tendency to consider women as subordinates to men has led to a perception of justification for wife battery as a form of disciplinary measure. It is seen as a private matter and as such consideration is given to the family, culture and religion at the expense of women in most societies (Gupta et al., 2013; Abeya et al., 2012; Carbone-Lopez, 2013; Archampong, 2010; Bamiwuye & Odimegwu, 2014; Chepuka, 2013; Adjiwanou & LeGrand, 2014; Jewkes & Morrell, 2010; Barnett et al., 2005). The most widespread form of domestic violence is wife battery which is prevalent in families with low income and unemployment, are isolated from kin and community, and particularly those experiencing a prevalence of high job losses in cities (Williams, 2009; Human Rights Watch, 2008; Kohler & Cambria, 2009; Finnbogadottir et al., 2014; Somasundaram & Sivayokan, 2013; Cunradi et al., 2011). Globally, wife battery is the most common type of violence against women and its worldwide prevalence is estimated to be between 10% to 70% (UN, 2006; Uthman et al., 2009; Mishra et al., 2014; Rapp et al., 2012; Bhatta, 2014; Adebayo, 2014; Ankama et al., 2014; Adu-gyamfi, 2014; Colombini et al., 2013). The former United Nations' Secretary-General, Kofi Annan opines that wife battery is most pervasive and knows no boundaries of geography, culture or wealth, thus making it a global problem. It is present everywhere, regardless of culture, ethnicity and socioeconomic status (Pool et al., 2014).

Wife battery is a serious violation of human rights which is not often discussed openly in society although it raises a lot of concerns globally (Quarm, 2009). As a result, it is very difficult to obtain accurate data on forms of wife battery due to factors like family privacy and the reluctance of law enforcement agents towards family disputes (Lohman, Neppl, Senia, & Schofield, 2013). It is also indicated that wife battery is the most under-reported of all crimes which is linked to the belief that battery is normal in marriages (Chepuka, 2013; Bhatta, 2014; Adu-gyamfi, 2014; Gupta et al., 2013; Stark et al., 2013; Bamiwuye & Odimegwu, 2014; Jirapramukpitak et al., 2011; Buzawa et al., 2011). Similarly, some researchers think that cases of domestic violence, particularly wife battery, are not reported because of the stigma, shame, fear of retaliation and the potential loss of custody of children as construed by women (Awang & Hariharan, 2011; Shrestha, 2014; Adjiwanou & LeGrand, 2014; Kuijpers et al., 2012; Rapp et al., 2012: Takyi & Mann, 2006). It is important to note that no one has immunity to battery. The circumstances at various environments can trigger battery as such victims might have different experiences due to their economic status, geographical location, family roles as well as community ties. For the purposes of policy and interventions, it is imperative to look at these causal factors as they exist differently among people in the communities.

Battered women are often in great danger in the place which is supposed to be a safe haven for them and their children. For many women, the supposed haven becomes a place they are battered by their husbands. Those victimized suffer physically and psychologically which may lead to health complications (Chepuka, 2013; Olsen et al., 2014; Shabila et al., 2014; Andersson et al., 2011; Dibaba et al., 2013; Ankama et al., 2014). Their human rights are denied and their lives are stolen from them through violence. Ghana's Parliament, for instance, passed the Domestic Violence Bill (DVB) into law in 2007 but domestic violence in the country is still on the increase (Adu-gyamfi, 2014; Pool et al., 2014; Ankama et al., 2014; Archampong, 2010; Cox et al., 2013).

RESEARCH METHOD

The study adopted a qualitative method. Data and information for this paper were initially collected in 2014 as part of a study on domestic violence and its impact on the status of married wives in Tamale Metropolis Ghana. The unit of analysis of this study was married women in Tamale who were victims of battery and have reported to the Domestic Violence and Victim Support Unit (DOVVSU) of the Ghana Police Service in Tamale Ghana. Out of 60 women, only 20 were suitable for this research. The authors conducted interview with 20 respondents and key informants, mainly officers of DOVVSU and social workers in Tamale. This was complemented with secondary materials from journal articles, books and the Internet. This paper intends to compare the data with relevant literature on the Malaysian perspective.

FORMS OF BATTERY IN GHANA

From the interviews, several themes have been identified based on the respondents' experience. To facilitate better understanding of the extent of wife battery in the Metropolis, efforts were made to identify the themes contained in different acts of physical violence like kicking, biting, or hitting with a fist, each of which contained a single form of violence. Other themes of physical battery assessed include pulling hair and dragging around the room. Other themes generated include deprivation of basic needs like withholding resources to punish the wife, neglecting the wife and children by refusing to provide money for food, school fees and maintenance of the household, preventing the wife from working as well as frivolous spending of family's meagre income. Some other themes include women feeling nervous, fearful, distressed, stressed out, having recurrent nightmares, having difficulty in sleeping and eating, lack of concentration, feeling hopelessness and losing sense of self. These themes were grouped under broad headings to include physical, economic, emotional, sexual and traditional battering as presented below.

a) *Physical Battery*

The term "physical battering" is used to include all assault with either an object or the fist by the husband on the respondents, including repeated blows inflicted just to cause harm. The respondents described this as intentional and unwanted contact by the husbands where the husbands use an object to cause physical pain in order to gain control and compliance over them. This sort of battery experienced by respondents includes punching, kicking, biting, being thrown objects at, pulling of hair, choking, pushing and slapping.

The study reveals that wife battery is extremely common in the area and only causes outrage if it endangers the life of the wife. This reveals a widespread belief in the community that it is the husband's right to beat his wife so long as it is to correct her, for instance, if the woman refuses to obey the orders of the husband as stated by the respondent above. This belief system fills them with self-blame, believing that their actions have caused the battery they suffer. After battery, the majority of the respondents think it is over but the batterer normally repeats the act without paying heed to any plead for mercy if there is any. Maliya (39) had this to share:

> He started to hit me with his strong hands and leg till I fell on the carpet and he stopped he waited for me to get up but I never so he took me up, tore all the cloths I ...yes I was almost naked he hit me and kicked me with his leg ... till I fell again ... I couldn't tell how long ... It was close to I do not know... and he stopped.

These attacks can range from bruising to death and according to Maliya, it starts with simple contacts which escalate into more frequent and serious battery. Most of the respondents attributed this act of violence to their economic and emotional dependence upon the batterer; as such they feel powerless to change their condition.

b) Economic Battery

This occurs when the husband uses money and other resources as a way to control the wife. Economic battery as revealed by the respondents includes taking merchandise on credit without paying, controlling resources and pretending to be protective, not paying children's school fees, making them feel guilty about their financial situation, borrowing without paying back and so on. Pagwuni (42) told the researcher that:

> I tried to please him by giving him some of the cash I make from my sales to boost his business, expand the business but he uses the money for luxury and on young girls lavishly, I give the money with the hope that these quarrels will stop but he will not stop I resorted to...

Other forms of battery the majority of the respondents mentioned were deprivation of the basic or essential needs like withholding resources as punishment, neglecting the wife and children by refusing to provide money for food, school fees and maintenance of the household, preventing the wife from going to the market or working or going about her normal business activities or being part of any income generating association (community based organizations), intentionally spending the wife's money or earnings just to destroy her business in order to make her dependent on him, lavishing wife's scarce earnings on concubines at the expense of wife and children. One of the respondents, Filomina (40) reported that:

> My husband started to hit me each time I questioned him about where he had been or how he spent his money and always complain no money no money yes for our upkeep. I also heard rumours from several neighbours and some of my friends that my husband has a concubine.

Another reported of her kiosk being locked with a different padlock and her chairs destroyed by the husband just to prevent her from earning her own income. Such actions and the economic dependence of women trap many of them in battery relationships. For instance, most of the battered women who do not hold paying jobs perceive themselves as incapable of living independently and therefore need the husband at all costs. Many believe that, regardless of their socioeconomic background and the extent of their economic dependence, ultimately they are determined either to divorce in order to establish an independent life or develop an endurance spring board.

c) *Emotional Battery*

Emotional abuse is any kind of abuse that concerns strong feelings rather than physical in nature which can include anything from verbal abuse to constant criticisms. Women are emotionally battered if there is substantial and observable impairment of their mental work that shows disorder in behaviour to include anxiety, depression, withdrawal, aggression or self-pity. One way to assess the emotional status of the respondents is based on whether their basic needs like adequate physical care and protection, affection, proper discipline and sufficient help to achieve independence and love are provided. Abuya (30) said that:

> Thing or issue that will make me feel better is for him the man my husband to accept the pregnancy, that will be enough for me I will be okay just tell my people and his people that he is responsible for the pregnancy so I can go to my people after delivery to stay...

Most of the respondents complained of denial of food, warmth and sleep; sleep deprivation is one form of torture. These types of torture often occur when the husband makes comments to frighten the wife, lower her self-esteem, or control her behaviour. Other behaviours identified by respondents as hurting their feelings include name-calling, yelling at them, controlling their way of life, making them think they cause their predicament, threatening to harm them or taking a second or third wife.

The women stated that battery included repeated verbal abuse, harassment, confinement and deprivation of physical, financial and personal resources that affect their emotions which can be more unbearable than the physical violence. The respondents also stated that it is unbearable because their security and self-confidence are undermined and that the worst aspect of their battery experience was not only the violence but also the constant fear and mental torture. Pagwuni (42) shared her mental torture in the following way:

> Living in battery relationship is not as painful and stressful as the anxiety, I live in constant fear and anxiety because I'm always wrong and that brings negative reactions from my husband.

The respondents also mentioned another abuse that was emotional when the husbands tell them that their action was the women's fault and that they (the women) were the cause of the battery when they knew very well they were untruthful.

d) Sexual Battery

Sexual battery that occurred was the unwanted sexual behaviour like unwanted touching or violent sexual activity where the women could not complain, and restricting access to birth control or protection against sexually transmitted infections by the husband who does not allow the wife to say no when not in the mood. Sexual abuse against married women reduces human resources, affects productivity and undermines economic well-being which in turn violates their human rights, hence their status. The respondents indicated that the violent behaviour of their husbands threatened their health, socio-economic and emotional well-being as a result of exposure to sexual battery leading to infection of sexually transmitted diseases like HIV/AIDS, gonorrhea and syphilis. One respondent shared her experience:

> The man is humanizing he goes after other women when I talk about the danger on our health it is beating especially when I mention HIV/AIDS disease and our chances of getting it if he doesn't control himself, eei condom, I cannot tell him ooi I cannot he will ... where do I know it? I will be labelled ... [jagmelo] a prostitute.

There are indications that sexual battery is a health problem in the area which compromises the physical health and self-esteem of married women. As such, this leads to protracted long-term health related problems like chronic pain, depression and risk of unwanted pregnancy, sexually transmitted diseases and serious pregnancy related complications. Lukaya (37) indicated that:

> Battery for me was the worse in my life I had miscarriage on two occasions after his routine beating and was even admitted at the teaching hospital on these two occasion he blamed me instead of saying he was sorry and regret for his action for the loses he was even saying all sorts of nasty … painful things again.

Most respondents stated how traditional norms in the Tamale Metropolis deny them negotiation rights for safer sex and control over the terms of their sexual encounter, especially in the context of marriage. For instance, the tradition of bride price paid by the husband to a woman's family grants the man absolute power over the woman. It is common belief in the Metropolis that married women are not supposed to deny the husband sex so this practice makes it difficult for married women to talk about their rights; they have accepted this form of battery as normal in marriage. No matter the severity of the battery, husbands are always right over their wives if the battery is about denial of sex by the wife. One respondent indicated that:

> It is unthinkable for a woman to deny the husband sex, if you are battered over this who are you going to complain to, who will even listen to you or sympathize with you, what or how will you explain this, to disgrace yourself no [ŋun lee su Naama bale o kpanjogu] traditionally, your body belongs to him including your everything.

Other forms of battery that surfaced include forced sexual intercourse (marital rape) in marriage when the woman is not in the mood, sexual neglect (the man turning his back to his wife in bed), wives' lack of control over reproduction and prevented from taking family planning or asked for forced abortion. The majority of the respondents revealed of being forced to have sexual intercourse, and some threatened and harassed when they refused their husband's sexual demands. Kande (37) is one of the respondents who experienced this:

> It started when I delivered and he was making advances yes making sexual advances and I refused I didn't allow him

because the child I had just delivered I was still not strong enough but …

Respondents also talked about damaged body issues while eating disorder has also been cited to have long term effect on the women. These women develop problems with their body image as some of them are made to feel bad about themselves, dissatisfy with appearance and result in eating disorders. Filomina (40) revealed that:

> He had one day even bitten me no not intentionally, he wanted to kiss me by force so in struggling his teeth crush my cheek you can still see the marks the scar of his teeth-wound I was treated.

Stress and anxiety are often long term effects of sexual battery which respondents indicated have frightened them and caused them stress even after they ceased. Saanpaga (19), the youngest respondent, said she experienced chronic pain, tension, anxiety attacks and phobias as revealed in the quote below:

THEMES OF CAUSES OF WIFE BATTERY IN GHANA

The causes of wife battering in Ghana are many and varied depending on the types of abuse and location. Stereotypical roles and traditional attitudes towards women help perpetuate battery which constrains the ability of married women to exercise choices that would reduce the agony of battery. Below are some themes of the causes of battery that have emerged through the interviews with the respondents in Tamale.

a) Infertility/Barrenness

Although a nationwide phenomenon, causes of wife battery vary from region to region and from community to community. In many parts of Ghana, including the study area, the inability of a woman to bear children is a major cause of domestic violence. One respondent shared what the mother-in-law told her on behalf of the son (the husband), that the main objective of the exchange in marriage between two families is to produce children. Filomina (40) shared this:

> This woman is not appreciative with the two children we
> are blessed with and is always telling me to produce for she
> needs grandchildren and not showing off a woman who cannot
> produce children is just a waste of resources and family riches
> resources, which is not even there, 'my son wants you to make
> babies for him not fashion, produce babies.'

A woman's status as a wife declines in some communities or families when she does not bear children which may lead to battery or even divorce. The study reveals that wife battery is a sad scourge faced by women without children in Ghana irrespective of age, education, religion, class or tribe. Some husbands have "preferred" children so the woman is not only to bear children but the right kind of children. For instance, giving birth to female children is considered unacceptable to some husbands, particularly those from traditional homes. As such, men who prefer male children may batter the wife for the offence with either the second wife or a replacing her with another woman who can produce male children. The experience of Filomina is an indication that the inability of women to conceive a child could be an excuse for wife battery by the husband in the study community.

The respondents revealed barrenness as another cause of battery by the husbands. So women who cannot produce children for the husbands are suspected of barrenness and are treated badly which explains why women, in particular, are still abused. The belief in most Ghanaian communities, including the study area, is that lack of children in the family is the woman's fault or misfortune and exempts men from any accusation of being the cause. Consequently, a woman in marriage without children has little chance of survival and usually ends in wife battery before divorce or separation. Married women are always suspects whenever the issue of barrenness surfaces, even without medical check-up for both to establish the problem or as evidence. This is mentioned by one of the respondents:

> The cause of this behaviour is that my husband is planning
> to marry another woman so anytime I say I ask him about this
> lady he gets angry and to defend himself he attacks me out of
> anger he one day reacted rethought that 'yes I have gotten a
> better one' means that my husband has found a new woman he

considers better than me, in what way I cannot tell. When my husband started having an affair with this woman, I became enraged and once …

b) Domestication of Women

Most men who batter their wives do not want them to work outside or take long hours outside or in the market or do things that will make them independent. Such men prefer to have women stay in the house to produce children and look after the house. So women who are industrious and do not yield to the idea of staying indoors or at home are reprimanded violently. One respondent shared with the researcher that the cause of the problems at first was failed promise to allow her to further her studies after marriage but the husband wanted her to stay at home to bear children. Lagfu (40) said that:

> … Education, before we married he promise that immediately after our wedding whether with child or without child I will continue my education but he didn't want to hear his promise again did not want to fulfil so that was our first misunderstanding.

Lagfu indicated that after college, the second problem was the birth issue; the husband always complained about the wife delaying in giving him children in comparison to other couples who married at the same time. This means if Lagfu had also stayed at home she would have been having children like their colleagues. The husband told her that and she commented:

> Colleagues have two or more kids and we haven't because of my selfish ambition school school school all the time and that where will I go with my education without children all sort of abusive talks so this leads to him going for going after other women because I cannot give him many children at the right time.

It was clear from the respondents that the roles of good mother or wife are cultural norms which they widely accepted and internalized. This is especially true among Ghanaian families where women are socialized and highly expected to be wives and mothers. In addition, preservation of traditional family structure and values is highly endorsed in many Ghanaian societies.

c) *Sexual Gratification and Accusation*

The study reveals that, traditionally, men stamp their authority when it comes to sexual issues as married women do not have rights in that regard. Some of the respondents said that it is disrespectful for a woman to report her own husband of sexual activities perceived to be battery which causes them to internalize sexual act perceived to be battery. Besides, the women stated that after a day's work in the house, husbands still expect them, traditionally, to prepare the main family meal and to be available at night to satisfy the husband's sexual desires; denial normally provokes battery. It is even unthinkable of any normal married woman to deny the husband because it is considered a duty known to every married woman. The only time the women have rights over sexual matters, is when they are menstruating or nursing a baby. Such conditions exempt them from sexual intercourse because the husband cannot make legitimate advances for fear of criticisms. Kande (36) said her husband did not even want to allow her to breastfeed and continued to harass her in the following way:

> The cause of this beating is as a result of my refusal of his sexual demand, his sexual advances were turned down especially when I had the baby it happened during my first baby and happened this time, this time is worst I asked for divorce for the sake of my life I don't want to die now being in the marriage means losing my life I don't think it is the best for me.

Dora (40) also suffered the same way as quoted below:

> I was beaten...... He didn't allow me to to sleep whole night. He forced me to have sex with him and ...... me terribly. I asked why he was treating me like that but he just did not bother. I really felt so humiliated.... and so degraded. I am educated, come from a respectful family, and I do not deserve to be treated like this.

Moreover, promiscuity is revealed as another cause of abuse as some of the respondents often cited it as the cause of the unbearable situation they found themselves in. Some of the respondents complained about the husbands' usual suspicion of cheating and capitalizing on that as an excuse to batter them. The wives further complained and wished they could object to the extra-marital affairs of the husbands. The man marrying a second or third wife is another serious condition that most often degenerates into violence and eventual battery even though it is the lesser evil compared to being a concubine. As indicated above by the respondents, husbands justify their violent behaviour by citing suspicions of the wife cheating which leads to severe battery by the suspicious husband. With this, the superiority of the husband in the study area is maintained through the practice of polygamy and/or restriction of movement of women.

This case implies that polygamy may also contribute to wife battery considering the unequal power relationship between husbands and wives in marriage in Tamale Metropolis. The respondents with polygamous husbands narrated the sort of unnecessary competition the husbands create which sometimes leads to animosity between them and eventual physical battering of the less favoured wife. The negative reactions of women to the husband marrying other women are grounds for battery. The negative repercussion of polygamy for women are sexual and psychological negligence as violent rivalry of wives and if a husband is biased and takes sides to abuse one in favour of the other(s). Bonsudung (44) shared with the researcher the route of the battery as shown below:

> The cause of this madness and insults all the ... is that I resisted his marriage to the second and the third wives, you have not been able to cater for our needs all the six children are in school you are not able to meet their needs both at school and home.

When Bonsudung reminded her husband to wait until their economic condition is improved so that he can go for as many wives as he wants, he defied the advice and went ahead to marry a second and then a third wife. With the second wife, the husband only informed Bonsudung the day she was formally brought to the house.

d) *Ghanaian Traditional Beliefs and Practices*

The troubling aspect of wife battery is the traditional and cultural acceptance of battery as a corrective measure as well as the husbands' right to correct the wife. The study reveals that some of the respondents shared the notion that the husband has the right to discipline the wife physically. Their response indicate that any behaviour by the wife perceived not to be in conformity with the traditional norms about the roles and responsibilities expected of married women is a justifiable cause for battery. So in such a situation, the informants stated that nobody within the community would sympathize with them or intervene when battery is the result of disobedience of traditional norms. By implication, the privacy of the family is immunity for the husband from public criticisms, formal intervention from NGOs, the police as well as criminal charges. The practice of patrilineal system legitimizes the authority of the husband and as the head of the family who is supposed to protect and control the members with whatever means deem appropriate.

The interview with respondents reveal some common traditional behaviours and activities expected of married women like preparing the main meal for the family, caring for children if any, seeking husband's permission before going out, avoiding argument with husband and meeting the sexual demands of the man. Neglecting the wife and children are also the causes of wife battery as stated by some respondents. Some of the men in the study area paid much attention to women outside[1] at the expense of the wife and children and when the women complain of inadequacy of money for their upkeep it may result in battery.

---

[1] "Women outside" refers to concubines and mistresses who are not traditionally or legally recognized as their wives but the men are in intimate relationship with them. Some men hide it from (it is not described as cheating in the traditional set-up) the wife but others engage in such relationship openly and sometimes behave in certain ways to hurt the feelings of the legal wife. This sometimes results to the men making the girlfriends, mistresses or concubines their second wife without consulting the first wife. And when these women complain the husband beats them.

e) Economic Dependence

The study discovers that women who depend on their husbands financially have little or no power to make choices, take part in decision making and in the maintenance of self-esteem. In most cases, the needs of the wife and kids go unmet when the batterer controls the household income which is a manipulative tactic to control the woman from whom money is being withheld. In the context of marriage in the Tamale Metropolis, many women who are less educated and unemployed remain in abusive relationships because they have nowhere to go or what to live on as marriage is considered some sort of security. The majority of the respondents (17) depend on their husbands economically so leaving marriage because of battery means aggravating their precarious situation in terms of poverty, shelter and security. Lukaya (37) shared with the researcher how dependent she is and the difficulties faced with her husband:

> My income is meagre and irregular it became increasingly difficult to manage the upkeep of our household as the money that was being given by my husband was not sufficient for the upkeep of our four children.

The above quote shows that women depend on their husband economically, making it the biggest problem faced by many married women in many communities including the study area. As indicated by Lukaya, married women who have two or more children in the Ghanaian community with or without income depend on the husbands for the upkeep of the children even when they batter them. Pagwuni (42) complained of her dependent situation this way:

> My brother where will I get money to care for myself and three children when he least supports, as husband and wife we are enemies and he often swears he will kill me he threatened my life several times and for implication of battery, I feel worthless I'm nothing without him...

REVIEW OF BATTERY IN MALAYSIA

The literature review reveals the small amount of research on the topic showing the paucity of research on domestic violence in Malaysia or that the studies are in the local language and inaccessible. Domestic violence is a serious but hidden problem in Malaysia (Awang & Hariharan, 2011; Ng et al., 2011). The largest prevalence study on domestic violence in 1990 found that 39% of the women were physically battered by their husbands. In the Federal Territory of Kuala Lumpur alone there were 300 complaints a month against husbands who physically batter their wives (Rashidah Abdullah et al., 1995). The Women, Family and Community Development Minister reported the escalation of wife battery cases from 3,093 cases in 2005 to 3,756 in 2007 and more in 2008 (Sunday Star, 2009 cited in Ng et al., 2011). Wife battery in the country is seen as a private and cultural issue, however, things have started to change because NGOs have identified wife battery as a public issue (Amirthalingam, 2003[2]; Comobini et al., 2013; Roslina, 2010)[3].Recent literature Othman and Mat Adanan (2008), Wong and Otheman (2008), Jahanfar et al. (2007), Phillips et al. (2006), Jamayah et al. (2005) and Norasikin (2002) on battering in Malaysia focus on health and healthcare issue, prevalence of battery and domestic violence resources. There are several issues pertinent to wife battery in Malaysia that are left unexplored.

Ghani (2014) explores the experiences of domestic violence from the perspective of abused women in Malaysia and found most women either feel reluctant to disclose abuse or conceal those violence because of Malaysian perception on disclosing marital affairs. Apart from the concern about the children's well-being, they felt the violence is caused by them. The women do not want to be labelled as disrespectful to their men. In addition, the findings prove the existence of domestic violence in Malaysian families. Indeed, the interference of cultural values as well as religious beliefs of the people in Malaysia is greatly associated with the prevalence of wife battery. Ghani (2014) maintains that battery is perceived as surrendering oneself to God for spiritual assistance as one of

---

[2] Elsewhere see Amirthalingam, K. "A Feminist Critique of Domestic Violence Laws in Singapore and Malaysia". Asia Research Institute, Working Paper Series 2003. No. 6, July, retrieved from www.ari.nus.edu.sg/docs/wps/wps03_006.pdf

[3] Roslina bt Che Soh Yusoff "The Cultural and Legal Perspective on Wife Battering in Malaysia". Department of Islamic Law, Ahmad Ibrahim Kulliyyah of Laws, International Islamic University Malaysia. The Law Review 2010. Retrieved from http//www.un.org/documents/ga/res/48/a48r104.htm 19

the impacts due to domestic violence problems. Further, the women lack of understanding of Islamic concepts like disobedience to husband makes it difficult to disclose incidence of battery.

According to Women Aid Organisation (WAO) 2013 annual report, 153 women sought for shelter at the centre and the majority of them were Malays (66 women). The report focused on the nature and type of abuse and found psychological (98.9%), physical (95.6%), financial (51.6%), social (48.4%) and sexual abuse (35.2%) among the respondents which shows that the women are subjected to multiple forms of abuse. Furthermore, financial abuse cases recorded include a husband taking the woman's money, depriving her of money and also contracting loans in her name without any service. This makes it difficult for the women to acquire property on their own because they have been blacklisted. As a result, such women remain disadvantaged and are subjected to financial abuse whether with or without a job.

The reports indicate that about 35% of the women said that the perpetrator abused them for no reason at all. A large number of the women (50%) revealed factors like jealousy, suspicion and financial problems as the main causes of their predicaments. Substances like "ice", "shabu", and cough syrup were identified as drugs used by some men and the cause of domestic violence. For instance, most of the times there was a mixture of factors like 74.2% of the perpetrators were influenced by alcohol and 37.1% of the women came from a violent family background. Most of the abusers were intimate partners of the women.

In 2014, the centre received 169 women seeking shelter and the majority were Malays (76 women) mostly from Selangor and Wilayah Persekutuan. Throughout 2014, the testimonies and experiences of women survivors' stories of abuse were recorded. These stories disclosed factors, trends and gaps to help explain the dynamics of domestic violence in Malaysia. In 2014, the most prevalent form of abuse was psychological perpetrated by the husband. The stories recorded reveal multiple forms of abuse like psychological abuse (100%), physical abuse (95.4%), social abuse (56%), financial abuse (55%), and sexual abuse (34.8%). The data identified psychological abuse as the most common form of domestic violence, impacting adversely like physical violence. Financial abuse was also rampant at 55% as most of the women shared that their husbands take their money without providing them with the financial means to take care of the family. It is revealed that some abusive husbands also took financial loans in their wive's name and did not subsequently service those loans. These women are disadvantaged economically even though gainfully employed, thereby restricting their financial independence even after leaving the abusive situation. The shelter attended to 1,740 calls during 2014 most of which were on issues of domestic violence. The majority of the clients were from Klang Valley, Johore, Negri Sembilan and Perak. The shelter also had 111 women counselled face-to-face on issues of battering.

Wong and Othman (2008) looked at the importance of early detection and prevention of battery in Selangor with 710 female respondents attending eight Primary Health Care Clinics. This study examined the relationship existing among ethnicity, income levels, education levels and partner's abuse of substance of adult patients and wife battering screening. Based on ethnicity, the study found that almost 58% of female patients screened were Indians, 32.5% Malays and 10% Chinese. The study discovered high incidence of battery among low income group while middle and high income earners revealed 22.5% and 5% respectively. In this study, more than 90% of the respondents disapproved men's right to batter their wife and one third of the female patients said they would not tell anybody, including doctors about the abusive relationships. Studies show that wife battery is experienced by women across ethnic and religious groups in Malaysia with different levels of education and economic backgrounds (Ng et al., 2011; Yut-Lin & Othman, 2008; Othman & Mat 2008; Awang & Hariharan, 2011).

Similarly, Othman and Mat Adenan (2008) assessed the knowledge, attitudes and practices of primary healthcare providers in relations to the identification and management of domestic violence. The sample was 108 respondents; 61 clinicians and 47 nursing staff. The majority of the respondents (62.3%) perceived that battery among the patients to be very rare. Surprisingly, more than half of the clinicians (65.6%) reported that most of the respondents did not ask their patients about wife battery because they did not want to offend them since domestic violence is culturally perceived as a marital issue between the couple. Collaborative studies in Hong Kong show that traditional beliefs regarding family privacy, family unity and gender role pose difficulties to heathcare providers in their management of wife battery (Wong et al., 1997). Kamarudin et al. (2007) investigated prevalence of domestic violence against pregnant women in Ipoh General Hospital in the State of Perak. Besides, the study measured the risk factors associated with battering during pregnancy. The participants were 134 pregnant women and the medical health record checklist was employed during individual interviews with the female patients. Most of the respondents (61.9%) were housewives aged 28.8 and lived in rural areas in Perak state. Kamarudin et al. (2007) reveal 4.5% prevalence of wife battery among pregnant women in the state. They further recorded 17.2% of hypertension and 10.4% pre-eclampsia as risk factors linked to wife battering. The study found significant correlation among the socio-demographic variables – age, race, education level and occupation – neither with domestic violence nor with any of the pregnancy and delivery outcomes. Small-scale studies on aspects of wives experiencing battery yield some data on the pervasiveness and nature of domestic violence in Malaysia (Ng et al., 2011; Garcia-Moreno et al., 2005). Other studies reveal data on allegedly battered women seeking medical care at the three general hospitals; Hospital Kuala Lumpur (HKL), Hospital Pulau Pinang and Hospital Melaka. Between August 2004 and February 2005, HKL recorded 206 battery cases, thus 24 cases per month on average while the other two hospitals recorded 73 cases.

Phillips et al. (2006) examined the psychological impact of wife battering on non-Western women in relation to Post Traumatic Stress Disorder (PTSD) symptoms. The study examined 17 female respondents at a women's shelter in Kuala Lumpur, Malaysia and 17 American women seeking emergency restraining orders from the Philadelphia Family Court Domestic Violence Unit, Philadelphia. The study found that Malaysian women reported more incidence of battery after the comparison between the participants from Malaysia and the United States. The study reveals that the majority of the respondents were abused psychologically and sexually. The high rate found in this sample was consistent with rates found in the sample of women in Philadelphia. The post traumatic reactions were examined from these countries to expose the experience of victims from different cultures but did not find any significant difference across samples. It was found that battered women in Malaysia stay longer in the abusive relationships than their counterparts in the US. However, Phillips et al. (2006) failed to give reasons why Malaysian women remain longer in the abusive relationships than women in the US. The cross-cultural assessment of post-trauma reaction among Malaysian and US women on the severity of battery using Violence against Women Scale (SVWAS) shows that 93% of the women reported at least an instance of being beaten, 87.5% reported death threats while 66.7% reported threat with a weapon in Malaysia. This study further reveals that women from both countries reported severe levels of distress as an indication of psychological problems battered women face. This suggests that problems after battery are similar in many respects, irrespective of political, ethnicity, religious affiliation, geographical and cultural differences (Philip et al., 2006).

Ismail (2008) examined the perception of university students on criminal cases like murder, rape, armed robbery and battering towards women in Johor. The study focuses on students' awareness of crimes perpetrated on women. Eighty-three female students were recruited across different disciplines form Universiti Teknologi Malaysia (UTM). It was revealed that the majority of the respondents identified murder, rape, robbery and domestic abuse as types of violence against women. Most of the students agreed that it is acceptable for the husband to use violence as a disciplinary action against the wife. However, few of them disagreed and said it is inappropriate and unacceptable action. Ismail (2008) failed to get the feedbacks on the level of understanding of students about social and legal provisions for battered women in Malaysia. Jamayah et al. (2005) focus on women's disclosure of battery incidents with 94 women who have been battered in the previous year. The study found that half of the respondents preferred to keep the incidents of abuse to themselves, thus few report abusive incidents to the authority for redress. Those who cannot bear the situation leave home, are separated from their husbands or are seeking for divorce. The women identified shame, the children, wanting to keep the family together, love, feelings of dishonour and wanting to protect the family's dignity as reasons why they could not leave the abusive relationship. The study also reveals that some women expressed their disappointment due a time consuming divorce process, and no appropriate action were taken by the authorities against the abusers.

DISCUSSION

It is quite clear that Ghana and Malaysia are to a large extent patrilineal socieies where by traditional men are considered head of the family irrespective of age which relegates women to subordination, making them vulnerable to sexual, physical and emotional battery. As a patrilineal society, the controlling behaviour is shown in the socio-cultural and economic life of the people just to maintain the status quo of the husbands. The data from the field suggest that wife battery in Ghana is attributable to these socio-cultural attitudes that condone male domination and women subservient. The factors found in this study are similar to several other studies done in Ghana, Côte d'Ivoire and other parts of the world (Adu-gyamfi, 2014; Tokuç et al., 2010; Guzzo, 2014; Pérez, 2014). The review on battering in Malaysia indicates that at the traditional household level, marriage life is based on gender power structure like Ghana which gives rise to wife battery with its negative consequences on the socio-economic, health and emotional standing of women. The study reveals further that in marriage the woman surrenders her entire body and soul to the husband which grants them – the husband - the audacity to batter the wife if she fails to fulfil the traditional duties assigned. This findings is in line with others that relate to poverty and gender-based victimization and domestic violence (Clarke et al., 2014; Arisi & Oromareghake, 2011; Amuzu et al., 2010; Kuijpers, 2012; Amuzu et al., 2010). In both Ghana and Malaysia, a woman after marriage is duty-bound to care for the family, particularly the well-being of the husband and children. With this belief, married women endure battery and tolerate every challenge from the husband and immediate family members as a test of womanhood. This could be explained in light of traditional family life education which has supported the rigid patrilineal power structure that makes the husband the head to the wife and children.

Another explanation could be the mother's way of socialization, where the daughter is taught to obey rather than provoke the husband's anger, making the girl-child docile and submissive (Uthman et al., 2009, 2010). This encourages and compels women to submit to battery and acceptance that it is all right to be battered in marriage. Women who resist this inhuman treatment in Ghana are labelled as disobedient wives and are punished. A similar study conducted in Malaysia by Jamayah et al. (2005) indicates that those who cannot keep quiet and resist this inhuman treatment had left home, been separated from their husband or are seeking for divorce. All of these cause devastating effects on their social and economic life. In effect, the subordination of women eventually makes them vulnerable leading to the unappreciable position and status these women are accorded. On the contrary, Pierotti (2013) found that women in most of the countries studied were more likely to reject wife battery during the first decade of the 2000s. For instance, a study conducted in Johor, Malaysia indicates that most of the students agreed that it is acceptable for the husband to use violence as a disciplinary action against the wife. However, a few of them disagreed and said it is inappropriate action and unacceptable (Ismail, 2008). In light of the symbolic interactionist perspective, cultural norms and values are learned through the process of socialization to guide human behaviour (Harrelson, 2013; Somasundaram & Sivayokan, 2013; Wilson et al., 2014). For the symbolic interactionist, the meaning of objects to individuals is crucial because everybody acts towards things on the basis of the meaning that those things have for them (Harrelson, 2013). For that matter, the way individuals in Ghana and Malaysia perceive events and objects, for instance marriage relationship, affects the way the husband and wife behave. The study reveals the sad scourge faced by women without children in Ghana irrespective of age, education, religion, class or tribe. Some husbands have "preferred" children so the woman is not only to bear children but the right kind of children. For instance, giving birth to female children is considered unacceptable to some husbands, particularly those from traditional homes. As such, men who prefer male children may batter the wife for the offence with either the second wife or replacing her with another woman who can produce sons. However, this kind of battery is not seen in the review on Malaysia, even though there are issues relating to child bearing but not on preference.

Good health is important for women to be able to cope with the responsibilities as wives, mothers and as single parents before, during and after battery. Health issues include psychological as well as general well-being concerning access to food and support. The themes generated from the data on the experience of battered wives on health are consistent across the majority of the informants. The study reveals that battered wives experience a range of emotional and physical symptoms of illnesses like depression, anxiety, eating and sleeping disorders, pain and damage of soft tissues. Furthermore, the women reported lack of opportunities in making decisions about their own reproductive health; moreover the husband and other family members took control as final decision makers. Wong and Othman (2008) looked at the importance of early detection and prevention of battery in Selangor among 710 female respondents attending eight primary health care clinics. This study found that almost 58% of female patients were Indians, 32.5% were Malays and 10% were Chinese at those clinics due to battery related health problems. The threat of battery to health, women's rights, and relationships that may influence reproductive decision in maternal health care service utilization are highlighted by several authors (Bamiwuye & Odimegwu, 2014; Cox et al., 2013; Abeya et al., 2012; Belita et al., 2013; Adjiwanou & LeGrand, 2014). It is incumbent on a husband in the area to provide the necessary physical, financial and emotional support for the wife to access general and reproductive healthcare. So the men have decision making power in matters like usage of family income, access to health and reproductive care as well as contraceptive choices. For instance, the decision to seek health care in the Tamale Metropolis is often made by the husbands or the in-laws because of the structure of the social system. However, most husbands do not fulfil this obligation and so deny women access to general healthcare until the health gets worse even to the point of death. To some it is used as a punishment to serve as deterrent to those wives labelled as rebellious women.

The majority of the women in both countries are reported to have been subjected to battery for many years (three and above years) for reasons like fear, infertility, accusation of promiscuity and traditional norms which lead to violence and increased health consequences or even death. For instance, mental health problems and healthcare decision making are identified as threatening women's health status (Abass et al., 2012; Uthman et al., 2009; Shrestha et al., 2014; Belita et al., 2013). The severe injuries sustained from physical battery come with a number of adverse health effects and even to the demise of productive women. For example, the women experienced medical difficulties in relation to high blood pressure, bruises, wounds, broken teeth and bones and traumatic feeling leading to chronic health problems and poor health status. In the same vein, studies in Malaysia also found such disturbing health issues due to battering. For instance, Kamarudin et al. (2007) investigated prevalence of domestic violence against pregnant women in Ipoh General Hospital in Perak. The study recorded 17.2% of hypertension and 10.4% of pre-eclampsia as risk factors linked to wife battering. In corroboration, studies conducted elsewhere found that women encounter medical difficulties like those in Ghana and Malaysia in relation to cardiovascular, gastrointestinal, endocrine and immune system through chronic stress. Besides, they state that medical disorders of the women may be aggravated due to lack of access to medication, medical costs and attitude of health workers (Njuki et al., 2014; Ndong, 2013; Colombini et al., 2013; Lasiuk et al., 2013; Ryan, 2008). However, in terms of cost Malaysia may be different because the literature reveals few from the middle and high income groups suffer from domestic abuse. Wong and Othman's (2008) study discovered high incidence of battery among low income group and low incidence among middle and high income earners. Nevertheless, financial abuse in Malaysia is reported to include a husband taking the woman's money, depriving her of money and also contracting loans in her name without any attempt to service the loan (WAO, 2014). This makes it difficult for the women because they are blacklisted. As a result, such women remain disadvantaged and are subjected to financial and even health abuse whether with or without job.

The study reveals that wife battery has not received the condemnation it deserves in the research area because the effects are not expected to last long. As such, most husbands failed to provide supportive environment but rather resorted to acts that adversely affect the women. The majority of husbands in this study employed various tactics to attack the wives just to create emotional discomfort for them. Besides, the husbands engaged in acts that restrict their movement, denigrate, ridicule, threaten and intimidate as well as showed signs of rejection and other hash treatments. In comparison, the women in Malaysia also experienced major psychological crises as shown in complaints and symptoms like anxiety and depression. For instance, Phillips et al., (2006) examined the psychological impact of wife battering on 17 female respondents at a women's shelter in Kuala Lumpur, Malaysia and 17 American women seeking emergency restraining orders from the Philadelphia Family Court Domestic Violence Unit. After the comparison between the Malaysian participants and those in the United States, the study reveals that the majority of the respondents from Malaysia were abused psychologically and sexually. The high rate found in this sample is consistent with rates found from women in Ghana. The battered women in Ghana and Malaysia endured the psychological consequences due to societal least expectation of it being long lasting. Contrary, the consequences turn out to be permanent and affect the psyche of these women. Some of the conditions that affect emotions as mentioned include loneliness, distress which match studies done on understanding psychological distress among married women, male gender preference and emotional distress (Qadir et al., 2011; Lako et al., 2013; Clarke et al., 2014; Lasiuk et al., 2013; Zacarias et al., 2012; Malta et al., 2012; Meekers et al., 2013; Shrestha et al., 2014). For symbolic interactionism, emotions are central to everyday interactions which motivate behaviour, shape agency, contribute to self-control and social control and bear the traces of systemic disadvantage (Blumer, 1980; Weaver & Agle, 2002; LaRossa & Reitzes, 1993).

CONCLUSION

It is clear that wife battery occurs across all socioeconomic, cultural, racial and tribal backgrounds of women in Ghana and Malaysia. The acute vulnerability of women to battery may include a host of gendered factors like cultural restrictions on their mobility, interaction as well as differences in the socialization of girls thus they are not equipped with the same survival skills as their brothers. When wife battery happens, people notice what is going on but will not interfere because it is considered a private issue to be handled by the couple. Wife battery which is devastating does not have to be because you have actually done something wrong as revealed. It leaves women and children hopeless, isolated and at constant risk of serious dangers to life and property. The paper reveals four common classification of battery like physical, sexual, emotional and economic abuse found in both countries. Physical battery in both countries involves contact like hitting, slapping, punching, choking and pushing intended to intimidate, cause pain, injury or other bodily harm or physical injury to the victim. Besides, wife battering is found to include wide range of abuses like denying the victim medical care, deprivation of sleep and functions necessary to life or forcing the victim to engage in activities against her will. The abuse could also target the emotions of the women like violence against her children, pet and those closer to her just to cause psychological harm to the victim. To survive this hostile relationship, the women employed some strategies to accommodate the situation during and after battery.

REFERENCES

Abdul-Ghani, M. (2014). Exploring domestic violence experiences from the perspective of abused women in Malaysia. Unpublished Doctoral dissertation, Loughborough University.

Abeya, S. G., Afework, M. F., & Yalew, A. W. (2012). Intimate partner violence against women in west Ethiopia: a qualitative study on attitudes, woman's response, and suggested measures as perceived by community members. *Reprod Health*, *9*, 14

Adebayo, A. A. (2014). Sociological implications of domestic violence on childrens development in Nigeria. *Journal of African Studies and Development*, *6*(1), 8–13.

Adjiwanou, V., & LeGrand, T. (2014). Gender inequality and the use of maternal healthcare services in rural sub-Saharan Africa. *Health & Place*, *29*, 67–78.

Adu-gyamfi, E. (2014). Challenges Undermining Domestic Violence Victims' Access to Justice in Mampong Municipality of Ghana, *27*(1996), 75–91.

Andersson, N., Omer, K., Caldwell, D., Dambam, M. M., Maikudi, A. Y., Effiong, B., ... & Hamel, C. (2011). Male responsibility and maternal morbidity: a cross-sectional study in two Nigerian states. *BMC health services research*, *11*(Suppl 2), S7.

Ankama, M., Oguntayo, A. O., & Akuse, J. T. (2014). Obstetric Outcome of Pregnancies Complicated by Domestic Violence, (August), 685–694.

Archampong, E. A. (2010). Marital rape–A women's equality issue in Ghana. *Faculty of Law, KNUST, Kumasi*.

Awang, H., & Hariharan, S. (2011). Determinants of domestic violence: Evidence from Malaysia. *Journal of Family Violence*, *26*(6), 459-464.

Bamiwuye, S. O., & Odimegwu, C. (2014). Spousal violence in sub-Saharan Africa: does household poverty-wealth matter? *Reproductive Health, 11*(1), 45.

Bhatta, D. N. (2014). Shadow of domestic violence and extramarital sex cohesive with spousal communication among males in Nepal, 1–8.

Binahayati, B. (2011). *Perceptions and attitudes toward violence against wives in west java, Indonesia.* State University of New York at Albany). *ProQuest Dissertations and Theses,* Retrieved from http://210.48.222.80/proxy.pac/docview/865844637?accountid=44024 accessed on 15th July 2014.

Buzawa, E. S., Buzawa, C. G., & Stark, E. D. (2011). *Responding to domestic violence: The integration of criminal justice and human services.* Sage Publications.

Carbone-Lopez, K. (2013). Across racial/ethnic boundaries: Investigating intimate violence within a national sample. *Journal of Interpersonal Violence, 28*(1), 3–24.

Cecilia, Ng., Noraida, E., & Rashida, S. (2011). Our Lived Realities: Reading Gender in Malaysia. Pulau Pinang: Penerbit Universiti Sains Malaysia.

Chepuka, L. (2013). *Perceptions, experiences and health sector responses to intimate partner violence in Malawi: the centrality of context* (Doctoral dissertation, University of Liverpool).

Colombini, M., Mayhew, S., Ali, S. H., Shuib, R., & Watts, C. (2013). "I feel it is not enough..." health providers' perspectives on services for victims of intimate partner violence in Malaysia. *BMC Health Services Research, 13*(1), 65.

Cox, C. M., Hindin, M. J., Otupiri, E., & Larsen-Reindorf, R. (2013). Understanding couples' relationship quality and contraceptive use in Kumasi, Ghana. *International Perspectives on Sexual and Reproductive Health, 39*(4), 185–94.

Crissman, H. P., Adanu, R. M., & Harlow, S. D. (2012). Women's Sexual Empowerment and Contraceptive Use in Ghana. *Studies in Family Planning, 43*(3), 201–212.

Cunradi, C. B., Mair, C., Ponicki, W., & Remer, L. (2011). Alcohol outlets, neighborhood characteristics, and intimate partner violence:

Ecological analysis of a California City. *Journal of Urban Health, 88*(2), 191–200.

Dibaba, Y., Fantahun, M., & Hindin, M. J. (2013). The association of unwanted pregnancy and social support with depressive symptoms in pregnancy: evidence from rural Southwestern Ethiopia. *BMC pregnancy and childbirth,13*(1), 135.

Diop-Sidibe, N., Campbell, J. C., & Becker, S. (2006). Domestic violence against women in Egypt-wife beating and health outcomes. *Social Science and Medicine, 62,* 1260-1277.

Dutton, D. G., & Nicholls, T. L. (2005). "The gender paradigm in domestic violence research and theory: Part 1-The conflict of theory and data". *Aggression and Violent Behaviour, 10:* 680 –714.

Finnbogadotir H., F., a. K., D., & C., W. H. (2014). Prevalence of domestic violence during pregnancy and related risk factors: A cross-sectional study in southern Sweden. *BMC Women's Health, 14*(1), 1–13.

García-Moreno, C., Jansen, H. A., Ellsberg, M., Heise, L., & Watts, C. (2005). *WHO multi-country study on women's health and domestic violence against women: Initial results on prevalence, health outcomes and women's responses.* World Health Organization.

Gilchrist, G., Hegarty, K., Chondres, P., Herman, H., & Gunn, J. (2010). The association between Intimate partner violence, alcohol and depression in family practice. *BMC Fam Pract. 27;* 11. 72.

Gupta, J., Falb, K. L., Lehmann, H., Kpebo, D., Xuan, Z., Hossain, M., ... Annan, J. (2013). Gender norms and economic empowerment intervention to reduce intimate partner violence against women in rural Côte d'Ivoire: A randomized controlled pilot study. *BMC International Health and Human Rights, 13*(1), 46. 30 Retrieved from http://www.scopus.com/inward/record.url?eid=2-s2.0-84886742698&partnerID=tZOtx3yl accessed on 21st August 2013.

Hossain, M., Zimmerman, C., Kiss, L., Kone, D., Bakayoko-Topolska, M., Manan K A, D., ... Watts, C. (2014). Men's and women's experiences of violence and traumatic events in rural Cote d'Ivoire before, during and after a period of armed conflict. *BMJ Open, 4*(2).

Human Rights Watch. (2008). US: Soaring rates of rape and violence against women. Retrieved from www.hrw.org/12/18 2nd April 2012

Ismail, F. (2008). Persepsi pelajar tentang kejadian jenayah terhadap wanita. Unpublished bachelor dissertation. Universiti Teknologi Malaysia (UTM), Malaysia.

Jacob Dindiok Konlaa (2011). An assessment of HIV&AIDS prevention and management programmes in the Northern Region of Ghana. A Case study of the Tamale Metropolis and the Yendi Municipality. Unpublished masters thesis submitted to the School of Graduate Studies Kwame Nkrumah University of Science and Technology.

Jamayah, S., Napsiah, M., Zabidah, P., Elicabet, P. L. (2005). *Domestic Violence Against Women*. Proceedings of the international conference on gender and Southeast Asia, pp. 184-190. Bangkok: WARI (Women's Action and Resource Initiative).

Jewkes, R., & Morrell, R. (2010). Gender and sexuality: emerging perspectives from the heterosexual epidemic in South Africa and implications for HIV risk and prevention. *Journal of the International AIDS Society, 13*(1), 6

Jirapramukpitak, T., Harpham, T., & Prince, M. (2011). Family violence and its "adversity package": A community survey of family violence and adverse mental outcomes among young people. *Social Psychiatry and Psychiatric Epidemiology, 46*(9), 825–831.

Kamarudin, E. B., Sarpin, M. A. B., Zakaria, N. B., Rahman, R. B. A., & Samsuddin, R. D. B. (2007). The prevalence of domestic violence against pregnant women in Perak, Malaysia. *Archives of Iranian medicine, 10*(3), 376-378.

Kishor, S., & Johnson, K. (2004). Profiling domestic violence: A multi-country study. *ORC Macro*

Kohler, J., & Cambria, N. (2009). *"Family violence spikes here."* St. Louis Post-Dispatch April 17:A1, A4. In Linda, L. L. (2011). Gender Roles: A Sociological Perspective, pp. 265. U.S.A: Pearson Education, Inc., Prentice Hall.

Kuijpers, K. F., van der Knaap, L. M., & Winkel, F. W. (2012). Risk of Revictimization of Intimate Partner Violence: The Role of Attachment, Anger and Violent Behavior of the Victim. *Journal of Family Violence, 27*(1), 33–44.

Lawson, D. (2003). Incidence, explanations, and treatment of partner violence. *Journal of Counseling and Development*, 81: 19 -33

Malta, L. a, McDonald, S. W., Hegadoren, K. M., Weller, C. a, & Tough, S. C. (2012). Influence of interpersonal violence on maternal anxiety, depression, stress and parenting morale in the early postpartum: a community based pregnancy cohort study. *BMC Pregnancy and Childbirth*, *12*, 153.

Meekers, D., Pallin, S. C., & Hutchinson, P. (2013). Intimate partner violence and mental health in Bolivia. *BMC Women's Health*, *13*(1), 1.

Merkin, R. S. (2013). The impact of sexual harassment on turnover intentions, absenteeism, and job satisfaction: findings from Argentina, Brazil and Chile. *Journal of International Women's Studies*, *10*(2), 73-91

Mishra, A., Patne, S. K., Tiwari, R., Srivastava, D. K., Gour, N., & Bansal, M. (2014). A cross-sectional study to find out the prevalence of different types of domestic violence in Gwalior city and to identify the various risk and protective factors for domestic violence. *Indian journal of community medicine: official publication of Indian Association of Preventive & Social Medicine*, *39*(1), 21

Norasikin, M. (2002). Domestic violence against women: The prevalence of domestic violence and factors associated with it among women who seek treatment at Hospital Pontian Outpatient department Malaysia. In Abdul-Ghani, M. (2014). *Exploring domestic violence experiences from the perspective of abused women in Malaysia*. Unpublished Doctoral dissertation, Loughborough University.

Olsen, A., Banwell, C., & Madden, A. (2014). Contraception, punishment and women who use drugs. *BMC Women's Health*, *14*, 5.

Othman, S., & Adenan, N. A. M. (2008). Domestic violence management in Malaysia: A survey on the primary health care providers. *Asia Pacific family medicine*, *7*(1), 2.

Othman, S., & Mat NA (2008). *Domestic violence management in Malaysia: A survey on the primary health care providers*, Asia Pacific. *Fam Med*, 7(1); 2.

Paula, N. (2010). *Domestic Violence and Psychology; A Critical Perspective*. USA and Canada: Routledge, pp. 22-34

Phillips, K. E., Rosen, G. M., Zoellner, L. A., & Feeny, N. C. (2006). A cross-cultural assessment of posttrauma reactions among Malaysian and US women reporting partner abuse. *Journal of family violence*, *21*(4), 259-262.

Pool, M. S., Otupiri, E., Owusu-Dabo, E., de Jonge, A., & Agyemang, C. (2014). Physical violence during pregnancy and pregnancy outcomes in Ghana. *BMC Pregnancy and Childbirth*, *14*(1), 71.

Quarm, E. M. (2009). Domestic violence law in Ghana: Analysis of the actors and strategies involved in setting the public policy agenda.

Rashidah Abdulah, Rita Raj-Hashim & Gabriele Schmitt, (1995). Battered Women in Malaysia, Prevalence, Problems and Public Attitudes. Malaysia: Women's Aid Organisation

Rapp, D., Zoch, B., Khan, M. M. H., Pollmann, T., & Krämer, A. (2012). Association between gap in spousal education and domestic violence in India and Bangladesh. *BMC Public Health*, *12*, 467.

Rezaeian, M. (2010). Suicide among young Middle Eastern Muslim females: The perspective of an Iranian epidemiologist. *Crisis: The Journal of Crisis Intervention and Suicide Prevention*, *31*(1), 36

Salazar, M., & Ohman, A. (2014). Who is using the morning-after pill? Inequalities in emergency contraception use among ever partnered Nicaraguan women; findings from a national survey. *International Journal for Equity in Health*, *13*(1), 61.

Shabila, N. P., Saleh, A. M., & Jawad, R. K. (2014). Women's perspectives of female genital cutting: Q-methodology. *BMC women's health*, *14*(1), 11

Shrestha, B., Onta, S., Choulagai, B., Poudyal, A., Pahari, D. P., Uprety, A., ...& Krettek, A. (2014). Women's experiences and health care-seeking practices in relation to uterine prolapse in a hill district of Nepal. *BMC women's health*, *14*(1), 20.

Shuib, R., Ali, S. H. A., Endut, N., Oon, S. W. and Shahrudin, S. S. H. (In press). A country level study of women's wellbeing and domestic violence against women. Unpublished ongoing research KANITA Universiti Sains Malaysia (USM).

Somasundaram, D., & Sivayokan, S. (2013). Rebuilding community resilience in a post-war context: developing insight and recommendations - a qualitative study in Northern Sri Lanka. *International Journal of Mental Health Systems*, *7*(1), 3.

Stark, L., Warner, A., Lehmann, H., Boothby, N., & Ager, A. (2013). Measuring the incidence and reporting of violence against women and girls in Liberia using the 'neighborhood method'. *Conflict and health*, *7*(1), 20.

Susan, N. A. (2013). Influence of Domestic Violence on the Socio-Economic Development of Women: A Study of Eldoret Town, Uasin-Gishu County

Takyi, B. K., & Mann, J. (2006). Intimate partner violence in Ghana, Africa: The perspectives of men regarding wife beating. *International Journal of Sociology of the Family*, 32, 61-78

Tumwesigye, N. M., Kyomuhendo, G. B., Greenfield, T. K., & Wanyenze, R. K. (2012). Problem drinking and physical intimate partner violence against women: evidence from a national survey in Uganda. *BMC public health*, *12*(1), 399

United Nations (2006). General Assembly: In-Depth Study on All Forms of Violence against Women: Report of the Secretary General, 2006. A/61/122/Add.1.6 July. Retrieved from www.un.org/womenwatch/daw/vaw/SGstudyvaw.htm 12th October 2012

Uthman, O. a, Lawoko, S., & Moradi, T. (2009). Factors associated with attitudes towards intimate partner violence against women: a comparative analysis of 17 sub-Saharan countries. *BMC International Health and Human Rights*, *9*, 14.

Valentine, J. M., Rodriguez, M. a., Lapeyrouse, L. M., & Zhang, M. (2011). Recent intimate partner violence as a prenatal predictor of maternal depression in the first year postpartum among Latinas. *Archives of Women's Mental Health*, *14*(2), 135–143.

Verelst, A., Schryver, M. De, Broekaert, E., & Derluyn, I. (2014). Mental health of victims of sexual violence in eastern Congo: Associations with daily stressors, stigma, and labeling, 1–12

Watts, C., & Zimmerman, C. (2002). Violence against women: Global Scope and Magnitude.' *Lancet* 359: 1232 – 3.

WHO (2006). WHO Multi-Country Study on Women's Health and Domestic Violence against Women. Geneva: World Health Organization.

Williams, S. R. (2009). *Double jeopardy: An assessment of victimization of battered women in intimate relationships and the criminal justice system.* Roosevelt University). *ProQuest Dissertations and Theses,* Retrieved from http://210.48.222.80/proxy.pac/docview/305139651?accountid=44024. Accessed on 22nd December 2012.

Wong Yut-Lin., & Othman, S. (2008). Early detection and prevention of domestic violence using the Women Abuse Screening Tool (WAST)

in primary health care clinics in Malaysia. *Asia-Pacific Journal of Public Health, 20*(2), 102-116.

Wong, T. W., Chung, M. M., & Yiu, J. J. (1997). Attitudes and beliefs of emergency department doctors towards domestic violence in Hong Kong. Emergency Medicine, 9(2), 113-116.

Yut-Lin W., & Othman, S. (2008). Early detection and prevention of domestic violence using the Women Abuse Screening Tool (WAST) in primary health care clinics in Malaysia. *Asia Pac J Public Health,* 20(2) 102 – 116

NGOS AND HEALTH SERVICES: A CASE STUDY OF MALAYSIA AND NIGERIA

Mahmudat O. Muhibbu-Din

NGOS AND HEALTH CARE SERVICES

While the government is responsible for the health of its population, NGOs are among many other actors that complement or supplement the health services effort of government agencies around the world. NGOs' size, reach and closeness to the local people combined with their willingness to confront the status quo and, coalition building improve their ability to deliver healthcare (Michael, 2002). NGOs' unique qualities include flexibility and adaptability, resourcefulness and willingness to work with certain, humanitarian concern. NGOs' proven track record and the legitimacy they enjoy in the local communities are comparative advantages in health programming (Michael, 2002, Gilson et al., 1994), closeness to the community, ability to experiment and innovate in pattern of provision and financing and provision of high quality care at low cost in some areas (Gilson et al., 1994). Obstacles to NGOs' provision of health services are dependence on donor funding limits their ability to innovate to attack emerging threats, government's antagonism towards NGOs, and difficulty inherent in building NGO networks.

Lankester, Campbell and Rader (2002) enumerate jobs often done best by NGOs in health services. These include: setting up primary health centers (PHC); encouraging the participation of the community; and training, teaching and motivating health workers and communities.

Meeting local needs with programmes that are flexible and appropriate; using money, people and resources effectively; working in remote or difficult areas, or with neglected, backward or nomadic groups; integrating PHC and development activities at the local level; establishing urban healthcare and working among the urban poor are becoming increasing foci for NGOs (p.276). Davies and Foley (2007) stress the importance of partnership in achieving greater health outcomes. Health promotion requires partnerships for public health and social development between the different sectors at all levels of governance and society. Partnerships offer mutual benefit for health through the sharing of expertise, skills and resources. Partnerships empower communities to improve health and promote health equality and should be at the core of global and national developments (p.133). Such partnerships between the public and private for profit and non-profit organizations are necessary to achieving health security of the population.

NGOs serve as a critical link between the government and the community. Chowdhury (1990) illustrates how NGO healthcare reduces mortality and morbidity, helps government to strengthen its system by providing training to lower and mid-level workers (p.116), establish primary health centers to cover such areas as training of Traditional Birth Attendances (TBAs), nutritional education, safe water and sanitation, family planning and basic curative care. The NGO health education helps people to manage their health either by themselves or utilizing government health services. According to Family Health International (2010), the success of NGOs in Nigerian communities results from their tremendous role in health services and commitment of dozens of community volunteers.

Research shows collaboration between NGOs and MoH in health services improves PHC systems and creates better link between healthcare workers with existing services, pools of resources, strengthens supervision, fills workforce gaps and improves patient flow between services and facilities (Pfeiffer et al., 2010). Other gains of integration include system efficiency by linking services through referrals rates, while accelerating the pace at which services can be expanded. NGO's partnership and integration with MoH fosters better coordination that supports system-wide divisions and processes. Pfeiffer et al.'s (2010) study emphasizes on the relevance of collaboration and partnership among different actors in healthcare creating needed support for government health systems. According to Ruhl, Stephen and Locke (2003:76-77), NGOs have the technical expertise to translate highly complex scientific concepts into public health action steps that members of the public can readily understand. Also, NGOs' role in operational research (OR) reduces disease burden and improve healthcare.

The organized political involvement of NGOs in seeking to influence public policy on health is a relatively recent development in response to the state's ideological rejection of universal welfare model for public health in Malaysia (Leng & Barraclough 2007:208). The functional role of the civil society in the provision of health welfare services to the population has become a common practice since colonial times and is seen as providing assistance to the disadvantaged (Leng & Barraclough, 2007:210). "Several necessary health services for marginalised groups, too politically sensitive for government involvement, are provided by NGOs. These include HIV/AIDS-related programmes for gay people, intravenous drug users and transvestites" (Leng and Barraclough 2007:211).

CONTRIBUTIONS OF NGOS TO HEALTHCARE: NIGERIA

NGOs are deeply community rooted and oriented, and in fact part of the community, understanding the problems in the communities and are suitably positioned to address the health needs of the communities. For NGOs to enhance health security they adopt a result oriented strategy using CBOs, CVs and community health promoters who do house-to-house visitation, offer home-based care support, check on the people to ensure compliance on the approved use of health products, track fresh suspect and report new cases of infectious diseases, and assist dying persons with the right health intervention. CVs are first line of contact in the communities and they know who to report or refer to in order to ensure the sick get access to healthcare in the appropriate health facility. Sometimes NGOs move into the communities with medical experts as members of the medical team on the field to ease access to healthcare.

NGOs offer a range of healthcare services to different segments of the population covering the literates, semi-literates and illiterates using preventive, rehabilitative, curative and promotive strategies to improve the health of the people. Some of the beneficiaries get to know about the NGOs through their methodologies of advocacy, awareness campaigns, health education, health programming, sensitization, and social mobilization on different health intervention, distribution of leaflets, handbills, Training of Trainers (ToT), and healthcare services rendered by the NGOs. NGOs also impart behavioural change through drama sketches and role play disseminating information and knowledge useful for health security. Delivery of healthcare products and health education by NGOs play a significant role in safeguarding the health of the people. It is agreed by all interviewees - government, NGO health providers and beneficiaries - that NGOs contribute to the reduction in morbidity and mortality in the communities through a range of healthcare services, knowledge dissemination and information sharing.

The NGOs' healthcare covers numerous range of health challenges in the communities from tuberculosis (TB), HIV/AIDs counselling and testing, malaria, typhoid, oral rehydration therapy (ORT), immunization, cardiovascular diseases, hepatitis, sexually transmitted diseases (STDs), cancer, diabetes testing, referral, emergency deliveries, training programmes and other aspects of health and empowerment. NGOs are involved in the distribution of insecticide treated nets, reproductive and family planning health products in various communities. The NGOs also focus on child survival. Under integrated child survival activities, Amukoko Community Partners for Health (AMCPH) work on strategies that strengthen immunization, infant nutrition and prevention and control of diarrhea diseases, STI and TB. The NGOs work to strengthen the capacity of health centres by giving them training.

The NGOs provide knowledge on the approved methods on the use of healthcare products in appropriate ways that ensure the safety and well-being of the people. The NGOs survey conducted before and after their health activities shows reduction in mortality and morbidity rate in the locality where NGOs worked on malaria. Malaria Parasite Africa Fight Back (MPAFB) educate beneficiaries to destroy mosquito breeding sites, sleep under mosquito insecticide treated nets, and carry on with monitoring and evaluation to ensure these products are properly used. Health products like Insecticide Treated Nets (ITNs), reproductive health care products and family planning methods, birth giving tube tablets, and adult education in the areas of Integrated Vector Management (IVM) are distributed to the communities. The NGOs choose to work in communities where they can make strong impact. MPAFB pre- and post-surveys after health activities show reduction in morbidity and mortality rate. CVs have helped beneficiaries in fixing ITNs at homes rather than reselling the distributed nets or using them for fishing as it happened in some cases.

To raise community awareness and impart positive change of attitude to achieve health security, NGOs must work with community volunteers (CVs), community based organisation (CBOs), community health promoters (CHPs) or village health committees (VHCs). CVs support community beneficiaries in monitoring the use of reproductive health products and ensure family planning methods are appropriate for the individual in question and track people to ensure compliance. The CVs teach new method of modern family planning and they help people to access it. The NGOs work through the CVs or CB distributors who carry their bag and go from house to house for women of reproductive age and talk to them, advise them to take new method of family planning, bring them to where they can access it and track them when they are supposed to take new medication (drugs, or injection). There is a monitoring and follow-up strategy used by the CVs to ensure healthcare and track defaulters. This strategy is used for malaria control, TB identification of fresh suspect, HIV/AIDS management, STIs control, maternal health, immunization and diabetes.

The NGOs create awareness, voluntary counselling and testing for HIV/AIDS and supply of Anti-Retroviral drugs (ARV). Under the Association of People Living with HIV/AIDS (PLWHAs), the NGOs give nutritional and psycho-social support to people living with HIV/AIDs. Apart from the drugs provided by the World Bank, Global Funds that government give to them; there are drugs that the HIV/AIDS patients need to buy that most of them could not afford. The NGOs collaborate with medical personnel and donors that sponsor drug acquisition to facilitate drug supply to patients. This is supported by donations from NGOs and individuals to procure drugs for patients. An NGO, CEPI encourages patients to attend meetings of PLWHAs. NGOs refer HIVAIDS patients to available health facility. Knowledge dissemination about HIV/AIDS incidence, transmission and prevention aim to positively impact behavioural change of risky sexual habit among sexually active people. The NGOs work to alleviate the plight of HIV/AIDS patients in the communities. NGOs train counsellors, educators, CVs and CBOs to educate the people in order to sustain health services to those most at risk. The LLO educates the brothels and has been able to reduce the issue of STIs and other type of diseases among them.

NGOs work through community volunteers (CVs) to change the health of the community by supporting appropriate health behaviour. The community health promoters and volunteers achieve results in health security in communicable diseases (CDs), non-communicable diseases (NCDs) and reproductive health. According to CEPI, the CVs in one community identified a suspect dying of TB in a poor living condition in her one room apartment shared with her family members. The CVs reported the case to the NGO (CEPI) in the locality. The TB suspect was referred to the nearest DOT centre where she was tested and confirmed to be suffering from TB, given treatment and cured of TB. She later joined the NGO to work as a CV helping to safeguard lives from preventable diseases and deaths.

NGOs help to spread knowledge on immunization to the people through the CVs. The CVs and community health promoters (CHP) help in identifying children who really need immunization and if possible bring them to the health centres for immunization and when defaulting could track defaulters. The NGOs get the CVs together and train them for healthcare services. These CVs need to do house-to-house visitation to get the people to change their health.

Helping community people to safeguard their health is one major way NGOs through the CVs make a difference in health security. The CVs track individuals through house-to-house visitation. This has contributed in no small measure in preventing avoidable death within the community. The CVs work for the health of the community. They are empowered by NGOs and they know a little better than the common people and can push the heathcare workers to give appropriate care and services.

LLO, through education offered to sex workers, has reduced the spread of gonorrhoea and other STIs among prostitutes and their clients. This further reduces the possibility of conflict that ensues as a result of the spread of the infectious diseases. The NGO engages all stakeholders in meetings including the Brothel Managers Association, community leaders, police, bar members and nurses within the community in dialogues to contain the spread of infectious diseases among sex workers. The NGOs' dialogue with the stakeholders, updates them of the NGOs' activities and receives advice from them on how they can work better. Some NGOs use mobile clinics to take healthcare services to the door steps of the people. This enhances accessibility of healthcare to common people most vulnerable to killer diseases that are largely preventable. Other NGOs shift healthcare services to different communities in the State, increasing people's access to health that otherwise might have been inaccessible due to poverty.

Findings show that the involvement of multiple actors in healthcare is because health is so important that it cannot be left alone to the government to shoulder the responsibility. All stakeholders involving the government at all levels, the NGOs, donor agencies and the community need to collaborate in safeguarding the health of the populace. Healthy people are considered the wealth of the nation. Only healthy people can contribute to increase GDP growth and economic development. NGOs make drugs available at subsidized rates to ensure affordability of approved drugs especially in treating common ailments in the communities like malaria. NGOs discourage the use of quacks in the communities and with the increased patronage of PHC, the quacks in the communities are lessening.

NGOs enhance the utilization of government health centres especially the primary healthcare (PHCs). Most of the people at the grassroots level have lost confidence in the PHCs due to poor service provisions, unavailability of drugs and sometimes health personnel to attend to them. The presence of the NGOs not only discourages the patronage of quacks at the grassroots but also facilitates the increased utilization of the PHCs. This fosters a synergy between the NGOs and the government healthcare services, a collaboration between the government and the NGOs that improves collective health.

All NGOs have a referral link to government healthcare centres for services they cannot handle on their own. The extent of NGO's follow-up on their clients varies from one NGO to the other. Some of the NGOs ensure that the beneficiaries actually access health-care from government health providers, other NGOs' referral link is weak and only follow-up on beneficiaries they could. The referral link framework is necessary for health security. Health security effort is not restricted to NGO health care services usually fraught with limited capability but extended to government facility expected to have all that it takes to offer the needed health service. The role of NGOs in restoring people's confidence in patronising government health centres is instructive especially in the face of dwindling service provision and poor attitude of staff in government health centres.

Health-Guard Foundation (HGF), an NGO, coordinates the referral network for community pharmacist in HIV response. NGOs do referral in other areas of health like high blood pressure, diabetes, malaria, cancer and TB. The NGOs have monitoring tools that ensure health seekers get to appropriate health providers for treatment. Health Matter Incorporation (HMI) works closely with Diabetes Association of Nigeria with their office in Lagos State University Teaching Hospital (LASUTH). The NGO ensures that all people referred there actually get there. They receive report from the department on the cases referred to by the NGO. For chronic malaria that requires microscopic laboratory testing, this is beyond the capacity of the NGOs to treat. NGOs refer patients to clinics or PHCs for further management. With the support of well-informed NGOs, people could gain access to the non-user friendly PHCs. The people know the NGOs and the NGOs are familiar with PHC staff and sometimes are known to the bosses at PHCs, serve as ice breaker between the government hospitals and the people and in increasing people's access to healthcare.

The NGOs penetrate deeply into the communities through the CVs, the formation of community based organizations (CBOs) and village health committees (VHCs). The NGOs are well known to the grassroots communities and are the easiest means to access the grassroots. This in no small measure heightens the NGOs' achievement in health security. In fact, NGOs' successes in health security are through these entrenched structures facilitative of community participation. The roles played by the community influencers and gate-keepers are constructive in allowing NGOs entry into communities. Community dialogue and consultation with the people ensure the health needs of the people are addressed through health gap assessment by NGOs. This contributes to safeguarding of the health of the people. The health gap assessments usually form the basis for proposal writing by NGOs. But these proposals have to be presented to donor agencies for sponsorship.

There is a consensus that NGOs' healthcare services alleviate health threats and reduce unnecessary mortality and morbidity in the population. Thus NGOs' healthcare prevents avoidable deaths. However, one of the NGOs emphasizes that preventing avoidable deaths may be a difficult task. To prevent avoidable deaths is dependent on the willingness of the people to abandon risky behaviour that threatens their well-being as well as the educational level of the community. Consequently, NGOs are not only involved in knowledge dissemination, but also imparting behavioural change. The beneficiaries from the NGOs' healthcare services suggest numerous ways to improve the contribution of NGOs to health security. These include greater collaboration among all stakeholders: government and non-government, local and international agencies, philanthropists and community leaders in supporting healthcare provision; capacity building of NGOs, more outreach centres especially in rural communities, house-to-house treatment, and funding for sustainability of health care.

Poor feedback mechanism between NGOs and the government, lack of coordination between NGOs and NGO network, inadequate funding of NGO work, unsustainability of healthcare, suspicious government officials, corruption, bureaucratic bottlenecks, and donor dependence are major factors limiting NGOs' contribution to healthcare services. Low educational level, and socio-cultural beliefs in the population are other constraints. Effective coordination of NGO coalition and network, cordial NGO-state relations, NGO financial independence, training and capacity building of NGOs, dedication and commitment to humanitarian services by NGOs and the availability of more NGOs; good governance and scaling up of NGO work can help alleviate health threats and reduce disease burden in the population. This is necessary for health security.

MALAYSIAN HEALTH SYSTEM

Malaysia's population of over 29 million benefits from a well-developed health system, good access to clean water and sanitation. Life expectancy at birth is 73 years. The Malaysian health sector has multiple healthcare providers including the public, private for profit and non-profit organizations. The public sector provides 82% of inpatient care and 35% of ambulatory care, and the private sector provides about 18% of inpatient care and 62% of ambulatory care. The MOH offers a comprehensive range of services, including health promotion, disease prevention, curative and rehabilitative care delivered through clinics and hospitals. The NGOs provide some health services for particular groups.

Non-communicable diseases (NCDs) account for most mortality and morbidity in Malaysia. However, communicable diseases (CDs) such as dengue, and potential pandemics such avian flu, are major health problems (Judith et al., 2013:1). According to the age-standardized mortality rates by cause, communicable diseases account for 161 deaths and NCDs account for 623 deaths per 100 000 population (Judith et al., 2013:8). The number of reported dengue cases has increased steadily since 2000. In 2008, 29,335 cases and 112 deaths were reported (the highest in the country's history), but the fatality rate dropped to 0.21% in 2009 (Judith et al., 2013:12). Malaria remains a problem in Sabah, Sarawak and central Peninsular Malaysia, with some cases in 2008 in the previously malaria-free states of Penang and Negri Sembilan (Judith et al., 2013:12). There is a rapid decline in malaria since the 1960s to 25 per 100 000 and the mortality/ fatality rate has fallen to 0.4% of reported cased (Judith et al., 2013:12).

The incidence of TB has increased from the 1990s. In 2008, the TB rate was 63.1 per 100,000 persons for all forms of TB (16,335 new cases and 1,171 recurrent cases), of which 10.2% had HIV infection (Judith et al., 2013:12). Incidence of reported HIV new cases has declined since 2002. During 2008, a total of 84 630 cumulative cases of HIV infection and 3692 new cases were reported, with the decrease since the early 2000s attributed to multi-prong intervention programmes (Judith et.al, 2013:13). The NCDs dominate the top five 'burden of disease' categories. The National Health Morbidity Surveys (NHMS) shows the marked prevalence of diabetes and hypertension between 1986 and 2006. An estimated 11.6% of the population have diabetes; second only to Brunei among South-east Asia countries and an estimated 42.6% of the population aged 30 years and over suffer from hypertension (Judith et al., 2013:10).

There are four major risk factors for NCDs: raised blood pressure; high body mass index; raised blood sugar levels and abnormal serum lipid concentrations. The 2006 Malaysian survey (NHMS III) estimated some of the common risk factors. Nearly 22% of the population aged 18 years are smokers, with much higher rates among men than women: 40% of men and 4% of women in 2000. Nearly 44% of the adult population were physically inactive, higher than in several other South-East Asian countries and 43% were overweight or obese (Judith et. al., 2013:10). Infant and child mortality rates of 5-5 per 1,000 live births in 2008 is similar to statistics in high-income country coverage (Judith et al., 2013:13). Malaysia is one of only three countries in the ten ASEAN nations (the others are Brunei Darussalam and Singapore) with infant and child mortality rates below 10 per 1,000 live births. The MMR has dropped substantially to under 30 per 100,000 live births (Judith et al., 2013:p.13-14).

CONTRIBUTIONS OF NGOS TO HEALTH: MALAYSIA

NGOs support and coordinate the efforts of other organizations working on health issues in Malaysia. NGOs work in partnership with government agencies, the private sector, religious agencies and international organizations in delivery of healthcare. Malaysia AIDS Council (MAC) provides nation-wide coverage of community-based HIV services and serves as the common voice for the communities. MAC coordinates and streamline programmes for its partner organizations, provides these organizations with the necessary training, funds and other resources to implement effective HIV/AIDS programmes within communities in Malaysia. MAC works to reduce HIV vulnerability in key affected populations via prevention, care and support interventions.

Capacity-building is done through training, programme management, financial and technical support. Advocacy on policy matters with stakeholders (other NGOs, networks, government agencies, private sector/bodies) aim to create effective response to health problems in the population such as prevention of the spread of HIV/AIDS, eliminate discrimination, stigma and prejudice associated with HIV/AIDS, promote and protect the rights of those made vulnerable by HIV/AIDS, ensure the highest possible quality of life for those with HIV/AIDS and provide care and support to individuals with HIV/AIDS. MAC community-based outreach and education programmes are key in improving access to HIV prevention and treatment services for affected populations who are often marginalized due to stigma and discrimination. Outreach workers, a vast majority of whom are members of the key affected populations themselves, are deployed as peer educators to disseminate targeted information, education and communication materials about HIV prevention, sexual and reproductive health, medical and legal aid referral services, as well as safe sex commodities such as condoms and lubricants. The NGO organises training for outreach workers on behaviour change that covers drug use, HIV/AIDS, and counselling and communications skills.

In 2010, approximately 68,000 outreach contacts were made with sex workers, transsexuals and men who have sex with men collectively through the work of ten Partner Organizations nationwide, with more than 500,000 condoms distributed. The NGO also fosters support group for People Living with HIV/AIDS (PLHIV) where they can control and manage their health more effectively. The peer support also implements home visit programme, to complement the counselling services offered at the hospital.

The National Cancer Council, Malaysia (Majlis Kanser Nasional – MAKNA, mobilises resources in order to provide curative, preventive, research and support services to cancer patients and families, high-risk groups and general public in Malaysia and the world. MAKNA works to alleviate the financial suffering of cancer patients by providing funding to victims and families of people at risk. Under the scheme, 92 government hospitals all over Malaysia refer their cases to MAKNA for financial help. Its partnership with UKM Medical Centre to jointly operate UKMMC-MAKNA Cancer Centre not only achieves MAKNA's vision of establishes a centre for individuals who cannot afford treatment but establish the most respectable cancer centre in the region. MAKNA receives referrals from more than 90 hospitals and 150,000 cases have been helped and close to 100,000 patients have been treated.

MAKNA introduces the nation's first mobile mammogram unit to the local communities. This is to help women detect breast cancer at an early stage. This has increased access to mammograms as the travelling mammogram trailer is able to operate in various challenging environment in different parts of the country. MAKNA creates cancer awareness and education within the public and communities. It also organizes comprehensive exhibition materials and trains personnel who help to disseminate and share information that increases the understanding about cancer and its related issues including maintaining healthy lifestyles. MAKNA education team conducts breast self-examinations and puts on educational presentations and exhibitions to increase the understanding of cancer. Volunteers offer home and hospital visits. They engage in and help cancer patients and their families. MAKNA cooperates and collaborates with companies with CSR to help poor cancer patients. Partners are willing to contribute their time, energy, expertise and resources in order to transform cancer patients' lives.

Similarly, the Malaysian Diabetes Association (Persatuan Diabetes Malaysia - PDM) helps people with diabetes have a healthy and productive life. PDM holds talks, seminars, camps and others, offers counselling sessions with health personnel, conducts health screening, makes available medical products and device to measure blood sugar, sells the needles at an affordable price, supports patient in need, provides social services to diabetics and establishes a centre for dissemination of information on diabetes and issues publications to members.

PDM makes available products and equipment used by diabetics such as syringes, needles, and blood glucose testing machine, test strips and urine test strips to its member at prices which are below retail prices. The NGO provides free meters, strips, pens, lancet needles etc. to poor and needy people. The free healthcare products are to enable people to regularly monitor their health. PDM conducts free structured education classes for patients and paramedics. These classes will help patients and paramedics to up-date themselves with matters on diabetes education, patient care, etc. Knowledge dissemination is expected to improve the standard of patient care in Malaysia.

NGOs raise funds through donations, grants, government ministries and annual membership fees. They maintain good working relationship with corporate partners and external funders, conducting and coordinating fundraising activities and at the same time advocating health agenda to corporate sectors. The NGOs receive donations in the form of cash or bonds or share certificates from any persons or groups on behalf of the association and also to borrow or raise money and to invest the money for the purpose of enhancing the scientific study of and the cure for diseases. Support from donors and the public, individual and corporate giving ensures NGOs sustainability of health outreach programmes into communities. Partners, supporters and collaborators work to ensure NGOs' continuity and sustainability. This creates the path to meaningful change and impact on how financially-challenged patients are assisted in the country.

To ensure survival and sustainability of services, NGOs need to consistently find innovative ways to raise funds to help patients. Public donations, and contributions play immense roles in how NGOs' services are delivered and the extent of assistance provided. Malaysian NGOs use all social platforms to reach out to people and get donations/support for their activities to sustain the NGOs. The issue of sustainability/funding is no doubt a challenge to the NGOs. However, effort is targeted to ensure the NGOs' dream is kept alive.

MAKNA encourages individuals to organize their own individual fund raising campaign/internet platforms for MAKNA. This innovative strategy of raising funds is a unique approach in addressing NGOs' fund raising issues. This not only supports the NGOs in furthering their activities, it has the potential to unleash the latent skills of the individuals in other areas of human endeavours. This encourages capacity building and extension of support services to poor cancer patients. MLF is a charitable organisation supported by membership subscriptions and donations from interested individuals and corporations. Fund-raising events are held throughout the year to help support the foundation's work.

All NGOs in Malaysia work for better health through public awareness campaigns, educational forums and events for doctors, research into diseases, provision of laboratory services, and organize World Health Day. Malaysia Liver Foundation (MLF) conducts screening programmes, vaccination against Hepatitis A and B at subsidized rates and counselling. As a non-profit organisation, it provides services at affordable cost to patients, creates public awareness and understanding of diseases to prevent long term complications; provides information regarding prevention and management of diseases to public, corporate bodies, government agencies and medical practitioners; and works closely with government and non-government organisations to provide services to patients. MLF assists the government to gather epidemiological trends of common diseases which may reduce morbidity and mortality in the country. It also provides vaccination programme for target groups, public seminars with blood testing; provision of laboratory services to test patients; and advisory services to policy makers in developing and implementing health care measures, conducting research and development activities in line with national health policies.

Generally, NGOs in health services in Malaysia work to ensure quality healthcare and support for patients in various aspects of health problems like HIV, diabetes, Hepatitis B and C, cancer, heart attack, autism, etc. regardless of race, ethnicity, religion or creed. The NGOs promote the scientific study of the cause and treatment of ailments and use knowledge diffusion as a key strategy for diseases prevention, control, treatment and cure. They encourage health promotion activities by creating awareness programmes of diseases and ways to prevent and control of diseases. NGOs provide support and create awareness programmes on healthy lifestyle, for the among public and various communities. They encourage, support and conduct scientific and medical researches on diseases and promote innovative treatment approaches. They offer screening and early diagnostic services to enable early detection of diseases. The NGOs rely on community support and train volunteers to carry out health activities. Community outreach programme is a programme to heighten community awareness, encourage community bonding aimed at increasing community well-being. The NGOs create positive impact on communities' and societies' health services. They expand the facilities which will enable a wider outreach outcome, push boundaries to meet heightened expectations, and continue to innovate to keep with changing times and needs of the public. The NGOs mark world/national health days and events; organize conferences and seminars on health matters to improve healthcare in different areas of health. NGOs organise comprehensive exhibitions and train personnel to help disseminate and share information that help increase understanding about diseases and maintain a healthy lifestyle.

STRENGTHS OF NGOS' HEALTH SERVICES

1. NGOs' healthcare is run by individuals who have the humanitarian heart to help support the vulnerable section of the population to gain access to care and treatment.
2. NGOs foster financial support for the less privileged.
3. They increase general public health through health education, health promotion, awareness and advocacy through knowledge dissemination.

4. NGOs get to the hard-to-reach population in delivery of health services.
5. They bridge the gap between the government and the grassroots through various community outreach centres.
6. They increase community participation and support in healthcare.
7. NGOs engage multiple stakeholders in healthcare delivery including health professionals, the community, the government, and the private sectors.
8. They improve public health through referral link and access to healthcare.
9. NGOs are generally accepted by the community and in some cases, are more trusted by the members of the community in increasing access to healthcare.

WEAKNESSES OF NGOS HEALTH SERVICES

1. They have to depend on donations to flourish and expand services to the community.
2. They must enjoy the support of volunteers to guarantee community outreach.
3. Healthcare activities are usually concentrated in a particular geographical location.
4. Poor relations between NGOs and government may limit their success in healthcare services.

SUGGESTIONS TO IMPROVE NGOS' HEALTHCARE SERVICES

Generally, the NGOs in health services in Malaysia and Nigeria are basically the same in terms of contributions to healthcare, as well as the dynamics of their operations and reach. NGOs are community oriented institution that seek to connect the people with the government and bring humanitarian services close to the people. The NGOs have proved influential in improving the plight of the vulnerable population and increased the hope of the hopeless section of the people.

The activities of NGOs usually depend on their financial capability and strength to expand health services to the people. Fund investment and income generating activities are possible ways to improve healthcare services. Malaysian NGOs developed numerous platforms to generate funds to support NGOs' efforts, including individual fund raising technique on behalf of the organisations. This is in addition to other numerous platforms of raising funds. Aside from those who are once sufferers of a particular type of illness, or those have felt the need to render healthcare support services to the needy or to at risk population, it important for philanthropist organisations, individuals/groups to contribute towards improving the plight of the vulnerable in society. The government can intensify its support for the NGOs in ensuring sustainability of healthcare by this sector to achieve the goal of health for all in both countries.

REFERENCES

Chee Heng Leng and Simon Barraclough (2007) Civil Society and Health care Policy in Malaysia In *Health Care in Malaysia: The Dynamics of Provision, Financing and Access* US: Routledge Malaysian Studies Series.

Chowdhury, A. (1990) 'Empowerment through Health Education: The Approach of an NGO in Bangladesh' In P. Streefland and J. Chabot (eds.) *Experiences Since Alma-Ata Implementing Primary Health Care,* Amsterdam: Royal Tropical Institute, pp.113-120.

Davies J.K and Foley, P. (2007) Partnership and Alliances for Health in C.E. Loyd, S. Handsley, J. Douglas, S. Earle and S. Spurr (eds.) *Policy and Practice in Promoting Public Health,* London: Sage Published in association with The Open University.

Family Health International (2010) Nigerian NGOs foster a Caring Community. Available at http://www.fhi.org/en/HIVAIDS/pub/Archive/articles/IOH/ioh11/ioh112.htm. Accessed on Jan 10, 2010.

Gilson, L., Sen, P., Mohammed, S. and Mujinja, P. (1994) 'The Potential Health Sector Non-Governmental Organizations: Policy Option', *Health Policy and Planning*;9(1):14-24.

Judith H. et.al (2013). Malaysia Health System Review. *Health System in Transition, 3*(1), 1–103.

Lankester, T., Campbell, I.D. and Rader Alison D. (2002) Setting up Community Health Programmes: A Practical Manual for Use in Developing Countries, 2nd Edition, Macmillan: Oxford, UK, pp.333.

Malaysia AIDS Council. Available at: http://www.mac.org.my/v3/who-are-we/mac/overview/. Accessed on 9/7/2015.

Micheal, S. (2002) 'The Role of NGOs in Human Security', The Hauser Center for Nonprofit Organizations and Harvard The Kennedy School of Government, Harvard University, pp. 1-29.

National Council of Cancer in Malaysia. Available at: http://makna.org.my/. Accessed on 9/21/15

Malaysian Liver Foundation. Available at: http://www.liver.org.my/. Accessed on 9/21/15.

Pfeiffer, J., Montoya, P., Baptista, A., Kargianis, M., Pugas, M., Micek, M., Johnson, W., Sherr, K., Gimbel, S., Baird, S., Lambdin, B. and Gloyd, S. (2010) 'Integration of HIV/AIDS Services into African Primary Health Care: Lessons Learned for Health System strengthening in Mozambique – A Case Study' Journal of International AIDS Society, 13:3, pp.1-13

Ruhl Suzi, Stephen Mari and Locke Paul (2003) The Role of NGOs in Public Health Law, Journal of Law Medicine and Ethics; 31(4):76-7. The Heart Foundation of Malaysia. Available at: http://www.yjm.org.my/. Accessed on 9/21/15.

REPRESENTATIONS OF AFRICA AND AFRICAN SOCIETIES IN A MALAYSIAN NEWSPAPER: AN ANALYSIS OF THE STAR

Nerawi Sedu & Nurazzura Mohamad Diah

INTRODUCTION

Mass media is are factors that influence people's perceptions and understanding of the world around them. Mass media are regarded as sources of information about the world, its populations and events that happen around the world. Mass media, according to Baran and Davis (2006, p. 228), " ... have become a primary means by which many of us experience or learn about many aspects of the world around us. Even when we don't learn about these things directly from the media, we learn about them from other people who get their ideas of the world from the media." In relation to this, Punyanunt-Carter (2008, p. 241), based on his analysis on writings and studies on the portrayals of African Americans on television, states that "communication research and theory suggest that the mass media are an important sources of information about African Americans and media portrayals contribute to public perceptions of African Americans..." In this regard, Dominick (2013) and Vivian (2014) state that one of the functions of the mass media, including newspapers, is to provide interpretations of events or happenings around them. In addition, Dominick (2013) also opines that the media provide interpretations to the audience. Dominick (2013, p. 34) writes:

The mass media do not supply just facts and data. They also provide information on the ultimate meaning and significance of events. One form of interpretation is so obvious that many people overlook it. Not everything that happens in the world on any given day can be included in the newspaper or in a TV or a radio broadcast. Media organizations select those events that are to be given time or space and decide how much prominence they are to be given.

In other words, the images of a society in the eyes of the public or audiences, to a certain extent, are influenced by the media representations of that society. The images portrayed might not be the real images or representations of that society. This might be due to factors or criteria such as "continuity" and "reference to something negative" (Harcup & O'Niell, 2001, p. 263).

AFRICA AND AFRICANS IN THE MEDIA

There are many studies conducted on media portrayal of African societies or African countries in the media (Asekun-Olarinmoye, Esiri, Ogungbamigbe, & Balofin, 2014; Punyanunt-Carter, 2008; Franks, 2005; Ndlela, 2005; Abdullahi, 1991). Based on his analysis of "media coverage of Africa from the early days of the explorers of the so-called 'dark continent' ... to present era [as of 1991] of neocolonial dependence and underdevelopment", Abdullahi (1991, pp. 3 & 14) found that among the references used to describe the Africans were barbaric, noble savages, and terrorists. Ndlela (2005, p. 71) says that "African countries are generally given scanty coverage in the daily news of the mainstream of Western media, except when there is a big event going on, a pending catastrophe, or disaster." In his review of a number of past studies on African-American portrayals on television, Punyanunt-Carter (2008, p. 242) opines that:

Research on media portrayals of African Americans has found that African Americans have been frequently portrayed in stereotypical occupational roles ... with negative personality characteristics, as low-achievers ... and with positive stereotypes.

Compared to past studies and writings, the present study mainly focuses and analyses on how a Malaysian English newspaper, i.e. *The Star*, portrays African countries and African societies. Considering the influence of the mass media, such as newspapers, magazines and televisions, on audiences' understanding of the world and the significance of African countries and societies, news on Africa and Africans are regarded as worth publishing. For example, one of the reasons for newspapers to publish negative news on Africa is negativity is always assumed to contribute to increased sales of newspapers. Newspapers provide a variety of images and interpretations, positive as well as negative, of the continent and its people.

RESEARCH METHODOLOGY

This study employed a thematic analysis for analyzing the data. According to Braun and Clarke (2006, p. 79), "thematic analysis is a method for identifying, analyzing, and reporting patterns (themes) within the data". This method enabled the researchers to interpret the data according to the prominent themes. The themes were developed based on the concepts, phrases, or statements that appeared frequently in the data. The data for this study were news articles collected from a Malaysian English newspaper, i.e. *The Star*. *The Star* was selected due its circulation. It is among the most highly circulated English newspaper (print as well as digital) in Malaysia (The Star, 2014). The data were collected for the duration of five months i.e. from March 2015 until July 2015. It is important to note that most of the collected news were not gathered by *The Star*'s journalists themselves. The collected news and features were subscribed from international news agencies or foreign news media organizations such as Agance France-Presss (AFP), Reuters, Associated Press (AP) and International New York Times. All of the news were placed in the world section of the newspaper. Thus, the sentiments in the news reflected the news values of these international or foreign news media organizations. A total of 35 articles on Africa and/or Africans were collected during this period of time. Examples of attention-grabbing headlines are:

a. From rodents to medical heroes - In Mozambique, giant rats are being trained to sniff out TB and landmines (World, p. 34, 25 March 2015)
b. Routed Boko Haram fighters hiding in Lake Chad islands (World, p. 23, 14 April 2015)
c. Tracing Che's failure in DR Congo – Guerilla leader's diary reveals bid to bring revolutionary war to Africa (World, p, 40, 23 April 2015).
d. Ebola spikes again in Guinea and Sierra Leone (World, p. 43, 12 June 2015)
e. Militants unleash havoc in Sinai (World, p. 31, 2 July 2015)
f. Suicide bomber kills five worshippers at Nigeria church (World, p. 23, 6 July 2015)
g. Gunmen kill 15 in Kenya college attack (World, p. 29, 3 April 2015)
h. 12-year-old girl kills 10 in Nigeria market (World, p. 42, 25 June 2015)
i. Egypt cops prevent bloodbath in Luxor (World, p. 43, 12 June 2015).

The news articles were thematically analysed, focusing on the phrases or terms used by news organization in reporting African countries and societies. Some of the most frequently used words or concepts or phrases are terrorism, terrorists, Ebola, militants, extremist, and Boko Haram. Based on the analysis, the most dominant themes are:

a. Terrorism
b. Deadly disease-infested continent
c. Political and social instability

FINDINGS AND CONCLUSION

The data indicate that most articles portrayed negative images of African countries and societies, as compared to the positive ones. This present study only focuses on the most frequently published themes i.e. political instability, terrorism, and deadly diseases. Despite the existence of many tourist attractions such as natural zoo or safari, the data reveal that the negative news, such as political instability and terrorism, received more coverage. In other words, there were more negative or dark representations of the African countries and African societies. It is assumed that the negative news would be able to attract more audience to read as well as buy the newspaper.

The following discussion will be based on the most dominant themes that appeared in the news articles.

a. Terrorism

Most of the collected news articles focused on the issue of terrorism which is regarded as one of the on-going major problems faced by the governments in the African nations. Terrorist groups such al-Shabab, al-Qaeeda, and Boko Haram appeared in many of the news articles. This is clearly indicated in the following the quotes:

> Abuja: Present-elected Muhammadu Buhari on Wednesday vowed to rid Nigeria of the "terror" of Boko Haram after his historic election victory ... Boko Haram, whose rampage through northeastern Nigeria had left more than 13,000 people dead in six years, is Buhari's most pressing security problem. (World, p. 34, 3 April 2015)

> El-Arish (Egypt): Militants unleashed a wave of simultaneous attacks, including a suicide car bombing, on Egypt army checkpoints in the restive north of the Sinai Peninsula, killing at least 30 soldiers, security, and military officials said. (World, p. 31, 2 July 2015)

> Tunis: The curator of the Tunisian museum targeted by a terrorist attack says it is postponing its reopening, for logistical and security reasons. The National Bardo Museum in Tunis was scheduled to reopen yesterday for the first time since gunmen opened fire on tourists March 18. The attack killed 21 people, and two gunmen were killed by police. (World, p. 31, 25 March 2015)

b. Deadly disease-infested continent

This study also found that the most frequently reported news was Ebola, which is considered as a deadly disease. The following quotations indicate the dominance of this theme:

> Geneva: The number of Ebola cases has risen in Guinea and Sierra Leone for the second consecutive week, the World Health Organisation said. ... The number of health workers affected in Sierra Leone, Guinea and Liberia has risen to 869, of whom 507 have died, since the current academic broke out in West Africa in December 2013. (World, p. 43, 12 June 2015)

> Monrovia: In the marketplace and at the school gates of downtown Monrovia, Liberians spoke of their dread over the return of Ebola after the first case in three months emerged. Health authorities said on Tuesday a teenager had died after becoming infected by the deadly tropical virus, seven weeks after the West African nation was declared Ebola-free. (World, p. 38, 2 July 2015)

c. Political and social instability

The data analysis revealed that *The Star* frequently published news on political instability in many African countries such as Egypt and Kenya. Generally, many African countries that received the coverage are represented in the news articles as troubled countries. They are represented as countries troubled by political turmoil or civil wars. This is evident in the following quotations:

> Cairo: The United States voiced alarm at death sentences handed to Egypt's ousted President Mohamed Morsi and dozens of others, a verdict experts called a declaration of "total war" on his Muslim Brotherhood. ... Experts said the verdict underscored Sisi's vow to eradicate the 87-year-old Muslim Brotherhood movement, which topped successive polls between the fall of Mubarak and Morsi's presidential win in May 2012. (World, p. 20, 18 May 2015)

Cape Town: As preparations were made to remove the statue of British colonialist Cecil Rhodes from the University of Cape Town, white groups launched protests to protect what they see as their heritage. South Africa's oldest university voted Wednesday to remove the monument from its campus after a month of student protests against a perceived symbol of historical white oppression. (World, p. 32, 10 April 2015)

Undeniably, there were a few news articles on positive developments or promising trends and activities such as news entitled, "Rap-porters' get with the beat" (World, 10 June 2015) and "17-year-old accepted at all Ivy League schools" (World, 9 April 2015), but the negative news received more attention and were frequently published by *The Star*. The findings of the present study are consistent with Asekun-Olarinmoye, Esiri, Ogungbamigbe and Balofin's (2014, p. 83) conclusion that "... decades after that debate [referring to the New World Information and Communication Order debates of the 1970s and 1980s at the United Nations Education, Scientific and Cultural Organization] was rested, negative coverage of Africa still persists in the powerful mass media of the industrialized societies". In other words, the mass media still highlight negative aspects of the African continent in their coverage.

Based on the analysis, the findings of the present study are similar to the past studies although the data i.e. news articles were collected from a different newspaper published in different countries. The images or representations of African countries or societies were more negative than positive.

REFERENCES

Abdullahi, A. (1991). Noble savages, communists and terrorists: Hegemonic imperatives in mediated images of Africa from Mungo Park to Gaddafi. *Africa Media Review.* 5(2), 1-15.

Asekun-Olarinmoye, S. O., Esiri, M. J., Ogungbamigbe, O. O., & Balofin, A. (2014). The impact of international broadcasting on Africa. *Developing Country Studies*, 4(4), 78-84.

Baran, S. J., & Davis, D. K. (2006). *Mass communication theory: foundations, ferment, and future* (4th ed.). Belmont: Thomson Wadsworth.

Braun, V., & Clarke, V. (2006). Using thematic analysis in Psychology. *Qualitative Research in Psychology, 3*(2), 77-101.

Dominick, J. (2013). *The dynamic of mass communication: media in transition* (12th ed.). Boston: McGraw-Hill.

Franks, S. (2005). Reporting Africa: problems and perspectives. *Westminster Paper in Communication and Culture.* Special Issue, 129-134.

Hoffman, G. (1991). *Racial stereotyping in the news: some general semantics alternatives.* Retrieved November 30, 2015 from http://www.generalsemantics.org/wp-content/uploads/2011/05/articles/etc/48-1-hoffmann.pdf.

Ndlela, N. (2005). The African paradigm: the coverage of the Zimbabwean crisis in the Norwegian media. *Westminster Paper in Communication and Culture*, Special Issue, 71-90.

Harcup, T. & O'Niell, D. (2001). What is news? Galtung and Ruge revisited. *Journalism Studies*, 2(2), 261-280.

Punyanunt-Carter, M. N. (2008). The perceived realism of African American portrayals on television. *The Howard Journal of Communication*, *19*, 241-257.

The Star. (2014). *The Star's circulation continues to rise while others decline.* Retrieved December 6, 2015 from http://www.thestar.com.my/business/business-news/2014/12/01/the-star-keeps-its-momentum/?style=biz

Vivian, J. (2014). *Media of mass communication* (11th ed.). Essex: Pearson.

GOOD GOVERNANCE IN THE HEALTH SECTOR OF MALAWI: WHAT LESSONS CAN BE LEARNT FROM MALAYSIA?

S. M. Abdul Quddus & Sherrif Abu-Bakr Kaisi

INTRODUCTION

The Republic of Malawi is a landlocked country bordered by Zambia to the west, Tanzania to the north, and Mozambique to the west and south. Malawi's landscape covers an area of 118,480 km2. Malawi has a population of 13.2 million people according to the 2008 Malawi National Population Census. Geographically, Malawi is situated in southeast of Africa (Kachala, 2011). It is pertinent to say here that the population of Malawi gets formal healthcare services from three main agencies, namely the Ministry of Health (MOH) which provides about 60% of all services; the Christian Health Association of Malawi (CHAM) which provides 37% and the Ministry of Local Government (MLG) that provides the remaining 1% of health services to the people. Besides these, there are private medical practitioners, commercial companies, Army and Police health care centers which provide 2% of health services to their own staff and kin of the staff (Chirwa, 2010).

Since the health sector is considered to be one of the major indicators of national development, it is incumbent upon the Ministry of Health to act expeditiously and efficiently to improve upon and provide proper quality and quantity of healthcare service delivery to the Malawian people. The people of the Republic of Malawi want the healthcare services of

75

the country to be efficient, effective and equitable just like the way some country's health sectors are such as Malaysia's healthcare sector because it is tax payers or citizens who fund the public expenditures and the Government. Above all, the citizenry of Malawi relies on the public services like public healthcare administered by the government for the nation's social and moral cohesion (Awang, 2000: 185).

It is equally important to state that the provision of healthcare services in Malawi is conducted at four levels: community, primary, secondary and tertiary levels. At the community level, healthcare is delivered through Health Surveillance Assistants (HSAs). It focuses on preventive interventions such as nutrition, sanitation, and provision of health information campaigns. At the primary level, healthcare is delivered through health centers and clinics. It is aimed at improving maternal and child health and promotion of early treatment of common diseases. The secondary healthcare is delivered through district hospitals; they function to treat more specialized conditions. Finally, tertiary healthcare is delivered through central hospitals. They function to provide referral services for highly specialized conditions (Kachiza, 2005). There are four main central hospitals in Malawi which act as the topmost referral centers where specialist services are available. They are Mzuzu Central Hospital (MCH) in Mzuzu, Kamuzu Central Hospital (KCH) in Lilongwe, Zomba Central Hospital (ZCH) in Zomba and the Queen Elizabeth Central Hospital (QECH) in Blantyre. The QECH is tasked with the responsibility to offer referral services mostly to the population from the districts in the southern region and to all other types of hospital services (Kachiza, 2005). Most importantly, of all the central hospitals in Malawi aforementioned, the QECH is the largest (Mfutso-Bengu & Muula, 2002). Consequently, because of its size and importance, the Queen Elizabeth Central Hospital (QECH) has been chosen as the main focus of this study.

In addition to the foregoing information, it is imperative to say here that good governance in the health sector is defined as the structures and processes by which the health system is regulated, directed and controlled. It includes the obligations of stewardship – ensuring that the system is well sustained for the future as well as serving the needs of the present. Governance is done by the people in charge; their authority is matched

76

with accountability (Dwyer & Eager, 2008). Dwyer and Eager (2008) state further that good governance is important in the health sector of any polity because effective governance, if applied in hospital settings, will in no doubt remove barriers, give permissions, set directions, better allocate resources and enable change and or reforms that are needed in that hospital. Furthermore, despite the administrative structure aforementioned, this study is embarked upon because the Malawi health sector faces numerous challenges ranging from lack of service delivery to the general public to patient dissatisfaction; this despite having all the necessary structures for health delivery mentioned earlier. There are growing concerns in the country about the tenets of good governance in the health sector, especially with regard to transparency, accountability and public participation. These, among other things, are self-evident in the public hospitals in Malawi.

The paper is organized around the agenda of "good governance" proposed by UNDP and adopted by Siddiqi et al. (2009). The objectives of this paper are: a) to examine the system of service delivery in a public hospital in Malawi; b) to explore the factors that promote or prohibit good governance in public sector healthcare in Malawi; and c) to proffer possible solutions to existing challenges of quality healthcare service delivery in Malawi taking into consideration the healthcare service system in Malaysia. The data for this paper have been collected by using survey questionnaires (total 120) comprising of service receivers (patients) and service providers of the Queen Elizabeth Central Hospital (QECH) such as doctors, nurses, midwives, and paramedics. Fifteen semi-structured interviews were also conducted. This paper used the model of good governance particularly related to the healthcare sector governance (HSG) suggested by the UNDP and adopted by Siddiqi, et.al. (2009) as the analytical framework for assessing good governance practice in the healthcare sector in Malawi.

HEALTHCARE SERVICES IN AFRICA

The health systems in countries throughout the developing world suffer from insufficient financial and human resources, limited institutional capacity and infrastructure, weak health information systems, lack of comprehensiveness, embedded inequity and discrimination in availability of services, absence of community participation, lack of transparency and accountability, and a need for management capacity building (American Public Health Association, 2013). It should be stated here that the health systems all over the world are suffering from years of neglect (World Health Organization, 2009).

In many studies, insufficient healthcare human resources are often cited as the most important obstacle to an adequate access to care and a successful treatment scale-up; overloaded health systems alo threaten the quality of care and patients' satisfaction levels, which can, in turn, seriously lessen the chances of successfully attending to patients' needs (Kazianga et al., 2013). In the study done by the PHCFM (2012), it was evidenced that despite having high expenditure and adequate facilities in hospitals in developing countries, patients were often not happy with the healthcare service they received from public hospitals. The PHCFM (2012) further reported in the same study that different studies have pointed out that the level of public health services in different types of health facilities and hospitals varies and that previous studies in Ethiopia have reported overall patients' happiness levels ranging from 52% to 57%. In the same vein, the PHCFM (2012) also states that previous studies conducted in Bangladesh reveal that greater levels of gratification was observed in private hospitals than in training and social security hospitals. Likewise, the same study notes that in a study conducted in Malta in 1998, findings show that the expectations of private hospitals' patients for service were higher than those of public hospitals' patients (PHCFM, 2012).

Schellekens et al. (2007) note that with few exceptions, African public healthcare systems border on being dysfunctional. They lack the medical and administrative capacity to produce services efficiently and of adequate quality. A 1994 World Bank study found that 88% of every dollar of public expenditure on medication is lost to inefficiency, with only 12% benefiting patients. The situation does not appear to have improved. Public systems lack transparency, making them subject to corruption and fraud and are not able to produce actuarial data on issues such as healthcare consumption and key performance indicators for cost of services. Worse, the public health services that are produced benefit the rich far more than the poor (Schellekens, 2007). Additionally,

United Nations' Development Program (2011) note that corruption in the health sector of any polity is a reflection of structural challenges in the healthcare system as well as where it takes place within the healthcare sector. Furthermore, among the key reasons for corruption in the health sector of any country are weak or non-existent rules and regulations, over-regulation, lack of accountability, low salaries and limited offer of services (i.e., more demand than supply). This paper argues that Malawi healthcare sector faces similar challenges which jeopardize the quality healthcare delivery to the general public. Brinkerhoff and Bossert (2008) clearly state that corruption is perhaps the most dramatic governance-related threat, but in addition poor accountability and transparency, weak incentives for responsiveness and performance, and limited engagement of citizens in health affairs also contribute to low levels of system effectiveness as well.

The foregoing discussion suggests that the matters discussed are issues of concern because evidence from previous studies examining the experience of those involved in providing and receiving healthcare services, as well as studies investigating factors that shape the implementation of interventions, can improve the relevance and scope of systematic reviews for policy-makers and the healthcare service providers (Nagata et al., 2012).

A BRIEF OVERVIEW ON MALAYSIAN HEALTHCARE SERVICE

Jamaludin et al. (2013) stated that the healthcare industry in Malaysia has been growing rapidly and steadily since the beginning of the 1990's and has been identified as one of the National Key Economic Areas (NKEA) under the 10th Malaysian Plan (2011-2015). According to Castro (2009), healthcare in Malaysia has undergone radical transformation. Over the years in, Malaysia has been continuously vigilant about its healthcare system. Concurring with Castro, Shazali et al. (2013) also contend that Malaysia has been continuously meticulous about ensuring an effective healthcare system. The increased number of medical schools shows that Malaysia is serious about providing quality healthcare, not only to its citizens, but also to expatriates, tourists, migrants, and visitors (Shazali et al., 2013). However, today's healthcare industry is continuously facing excessively increased cost, declining profitability, administrative inefficiency, and steep regulatory compliance.[4] Shazali et al. (2013) state that healthcare in Malaysia is mainly under the responsibility of the government's Ministry of Health. They further note that Malaysian healthcare system is divided into two sectors consisting of both the government healthcare system and private healthcare system.[5]

As stated above, Malawi's healthcare system is quite similar to Malaysian healthcare sector; it is divided into two sectors, namely the public and the private healthcare sector, hence Malawi as one of Africa's underdeveloping countries can learn more from Malaysia. It is revealed by the Malaysian-German Chamber of Commerce & Industry, Market Watch (2011) that public hospitals in Malaysia deal with increasing workload and the public sector resources are stretched to the capacity compared to the private sector. This is similar to Malawi's case. However, it should be noted that Malaysia has better opportunity to improve the healthcare service delivery to its citizenry compared to Malawi. This fact can be demonstrated by looking at the economic muscle the former has compared to the latter. For instance, Malaysia operates mobile clinics and provide flying doctor services to remote areas. Furthermore, Malaysia imports technologically advanced medical equipments for its public hospitals, and it also exports some medical items such as surgical and examination gloves, dental and ophthalmic instruments and appliances[6] (Malaysian-German Chamber of Commerce & Industry, Market Watch 2011).

HEALTHCARE SERVICES IN MALAWI HOSPITALS

The Nyasa Times News (2013) notes that a healthy nation is essential for the development of a country. As such the government of Malawi has continued to put a lot of effort in improving the health sector of the

---

[4] Noor Hidayah Jamaludin, Nurul Fadly Habidin, Nurul Aifaa Shazali, Naimah Ali, Nur Afni Khaidir. "Exploring Sustainable Healthcare Service and Sustainable Healthcare Performance: Based on Malaysian Healthcare Industry" Journal of Sustainable Development Studies. Volume 3, Number 1, 2013, 14-26. ISSN 2201-4268.

[5] Shazali e t.al (2013). "Lean Healthcare Practice and Healthcare Performance in Malaysian Healthcare Industry". *International Journal of Scientific and Research Publications*, Volume 3, Issue 1, January 2013. ISSN 2250-3153.

[6] Malaysian-German Chamber of Commerce & Industry, Market Watch 2011.

country. In 2011/2012 fiscal year for example, a health sector strategic plan for 2011-2016 was developed. Strategic focus areas include human resource development; retention, strengthening supply chain, management for essential drugs and medical supplies; and construction and rehabilitation and maintenance of health infrastructure (Nyasa Times News, 2013).

Despite this report, most health facilities in the rural areas of Malawi have reported lack of electricity which is a major system barrier and recent assessments of the Malawi health sector demonstrate that there are a number of health system barriers that affect the delivery of the Essential Healthcare Package (EHP) including the delivery of immunization services. One of the major barriers in the delivery of the EHP in Malawi is the critical shortage of human resources arising from lack of strategic human resource planning and management, unattractive remuneration packages and the general underinvestment in the training of health personnel (GAVI Alliance Health System, 2007); also, there is an uneven distribution of healthcare resources in Malawi, with only 46% of the population having access to formal health facilities within a 5 kilometer radius yet 20% of the population live within a 25 kilometer radius of a hospital (Chigwedere, 2009). It has also been reported by White (2011) that there is always a long line of people sitting on the benches along the walls of the ward of the Queen Elizabeth Central Hospital Blantyre Malawi. White (2011) reports further that most of the people are mothers with one or two small children, who are occasionally very well-dressed adults, but that most of them that are sitting on the benches are poor people.

In a study conducted by Oxfam International (2008), their findings indicate that there are still three key impediments to quality health services in Malawi: access to essential medicines; access to health services facilities, which are further compounded by user fees, especially in CHAM hospitals; and the human-resource crisis. Furthermore, each day Malawians continue to suffer from chronic or treatable illnesses as a direct result of a lack of adequately equipped healthcare facilities. Whilst the government has made meaningful steps to centralizing health issues within its strategic plans, there are still many people that are unable to get access to the treatment and services they need.

Another study conducted by Changole et al. (2010) on patients' satisfaction with reproductive health services at the Gogo Chatinkha

Maternity Unit of the Queen Elizabeth Central Hospital, Blantyre, Malawi reveals that although the patients expected professional care, there was a reticence on their part about asking the doctors and nurses concerning the information they wanted to know. This according to the researchers could be due to cultural factors where it could be seen as inappropriate to question medical personnel. It is noteworthy to add here that almost half of the mothers who participated in Changole et al.'s (2010) study had never heard of any patients' rights before. This finding indicates how the healthcare service system in Malawi has neglected such an important legal issue.

Considering the above information and in the study done by Al-Hawary (2012) where he reports that previous studies on healthcare delivery have been anchored on traditional approach to assess healthcare service delivery, which according to him has been built entirely on the viewpoint of healthcare providers, care takers and the government where they analyze the health related statistics over a period of time, but neglect the patients' perspectives who are the healthcare service receivers from the hospitals. However, the views of the patients are increasingly becoming important in the evaluation of healthcare service delivery, and even if the views of the patients differ significantly from the concept of quality maintained by the healthcare providers and healthcare authorities, their opinions can be employed for meaningful changes in the service delivery system (Al-Hawary, 2012).

FACTORS THAT CHARACTERIZE THE HEALTHCARE SERVICE DELIVERY SYSTEM IN MALAWI

This study was embarked upon in order to examine the level of health service delivery in Malawi in general and the QECH in particular and what lessons Malawi can learn from Malaysia. Also the study aimed at investigating how health professionals (doctors, nurses, etc.) in Malawi perceive their roles and how their role perceptions shape their behaviour in a bid to explore the factors that promote or prohibit good governance in the public sector healthcare delivery systems in Malawi so as to offer possible solutions to existing challenges of good governance in the QECH.

The findings from this study have clearly revealed that ethics, rule of law, equity and inclusiveness, participation and consensus orientation, effectiveness and efficiency and responsiveness, information and intelligence, accountability and transparency, vision and mission characterize the service delivery system of the QECH with varying degrees. In addition, ethics as a dimension for assessing the health sector's good governance is found by this study to be wholly present at the QECH because the data reveal that the hospital staff adhere strictly to the oath which they swore to before they are commissioned to work as medical practitioners. Furthermore, rule of law; equity and inclusiveness are also discovered to be present in the QECH because the findings show that the hospital staff attend to their patients without minding the patients' religious affiliation, ethnicity or gender identity. The only shortcoming closely related to religious belief, ethnicity and gender is when the QECH staff act below expectation as they attend to patients based on their social status in society. Also, for the UNDP and the WHO factors such as participation and consensus orientation, effectiveness and efficiency, information and intelligence and responsiveness; all characterize the health service delivery of the QECH, but below a moderate level. Finally, accountability and transparency are the only two constructs in the UNDP and the WHO proposed framework for ascertaining healthcare governance that are found to be conspicuously missing in the hospital.

In addition to the above information, the vision and mission statement of the hospital, although present and well-defined by the government, are however not fully practised in the hospital and as such one can infer that the vision is only ideal on paper; this is because the original vision of the government for the QECH according to the findings of this study is to ensure that Malawi citizens have access to healthcare facilities and these facilities should be able to provide quality services to the people. These findings obtained from the qualitative data are in consonance with the findings obtained from the survey where the results on the construct tagged strategic vision in the questionnaire yielded a total mean of 3.70 for the six items under that dimension. To reiterate, the findings show that there are vision and mission meant for the operations of the QECH, but they are somewhat not fully in practice. One of the service receivers specifically stated that many times when he visits the hospital for treatment, he discovers that the hospital is devoid of essential drugs. This implies that the hospital is not meeting its vision which is to ensure that all citizens have access to healthcare facility from which they can get quality healthcare services; at the QECH the reverse is true.

The findings from both interview and survey data are in agreement with the findings of the study conducted by Lewis et al. (2009) where the authors report that poor governance is responsible for much of the inefficiency in the service provision in the health sector which in some cases have resulted in no service at all. These findings are also in alignment with findings from the study by Zere et al. (2006) where they report that the supply of healthcare resources to address the problems of healthcare receivers has been continuously declining in many countries. No wonder the American Public Health Association (2013) states in its study that there is a need for management capacity building in the health sector of developing countries including those of Malawi and Schellekens et al. (2007) also note in the study they conducted that with few exceptions, African countries' public healthcare systems border on the dysfunctional state because according to them, they lack the medical and administrative capacity to produce services efficiently and of adequate quality. Additionally, these findings are in total agreement with the 1994 World Bank study which shows that 88% of every dollar of public expenditure on medication is lost to inefficiency, with only 12% benefiting the patients. The situation does not appear to have improved judging from the data acquired from the interviews and survey with the QECH respondents of this study. Additionally, findings from the survey data show a mean for intelligence and information as 2.29. This is below the mean level and one can therefore conclude here that intelligence and information also do not characterize service delivery of the QECH. This is in line with what has been reported by the World Health Organization (2007) that much of the burden of disease can be prevented or cured with known, affordable technologies, but the problem is information and other forms of prevention, timely care or treatment, reliably in sufficient quantity and at reasonable costs to those who need them.

In sharp contrast however, this research findings do not agree with the findings by Zachimalawi (2010) that sub-charging patients before treating them characterizes service delivery of the QECH. Specifically, Zachimalawi (2010) reports that day light robbery is taking place at QECH, Malawi's referral hospital in the southern region, where staff members from the hospital's Dental Department are charging patients referred from district hospitals a non-refundable fee of K5,000. But the results of this study have contravened that report and this is very clear from their responses such as:

> "We don't pay money here for treatment the hospital gives free healthcare service to us"

> "I have never been asked to pay".[7]

a) *Bureaucratic Attitude and Unpredicted Behavior of Health Professionals*

Our data show that most of the QECH staff are friendly but there are also staffs who exhibit bureaucratic and unexpected behaviour such as shouting at patients while administering treatment to them. The findings show that the QECH staff perceive revealing their patient's secret to be a forbidden act and they are also guided by the rules and regulations of the medical profession which do not permit them to do such things. As a matter of fact, they said they have never done such a thing before and that they will never do it either. This is evident in the response of a doctor who stated the following, *"No, I cannot do that because it's prohibited and against the rule guiding my profession and the oath I took before I started work".[8]* Again, this study also reveal that some of the QECH staff are very polite while discharging their duties, although there are a few QECH staff who are not polite while doing the same thing. No wonder Kumbani et al. (2012) assert that healthcare service providers should endeavour to show empathy towards healthcare service receivers and at the same time provide care that is acceptable and suitable to all patients based on set guidelines.

The study further reveals that at the QECH, patients are only allowed to ask service providers questions to a certain limit. This implies that they are only allowed to ask questions relating to their health complaints but are restricted from asking questions that have to do with the administrative procedures of the hospital. The aforementioned findings are in agreement with the findings obtained from the survey conducted for this study where a mean of 3.07 was obtained for all nine items under the construct

---

[7] Interview 11.

[8] Interview

tagged "ethics" in relation to quality service and good governance in a hospital setting. These findings are in contrast to the findings of the study conducted by Changole et al. (2010) where their findings indicate that the patients of the QECH had expected professional care, but that there was unwillingness on their part (i.e. the patients) to speak about their own thoughts by asking the doctors and nurses concerning the information they wanted to know. The study however, has found that the patients are never restricted from speaking their mind or asking the health providers questions they need to know about their health status. Additionally, this study has also found that in contrast to what was reported by Berlan and Shiffma (2011) that in low income countries, many providers do not consider it their responsibility to listen carefully to patients' preferences, to facilitate access to care, to offer detailed information or to treat patients with respect.

This paper has revealed that staff of the QECH are always all ears whenever the service receivers need to know something regarding their health. Allowing the patients of the QECH to speak their mind or ask questions relating to their health is a welcomed development for the QECH authorities because as Mahmud (2004) rightly puts it, increasing people's voice and influence in the health sector is generally believed to be an effective way of improving the performance of health systems, i.e. increasing access to services of the most vulnerable and disadvantaged groups, which will improve the health outcomes generally and reduce health inequities among the populace.

b) *Lack of Transparency and Accountability in Service Delivery*

The impact of transparency and accountability on service delivery has always been an underlying motive in the literature on service delivery (Joshi, 2010) and in order for health care service delivery systems to function at optimal standards, the American Public Health Association (2013) notes that health systems should be effective, integrated, and evidence based, embracing activities to promote health, prevent diseases, and offer diagnosis and treatment; be based on principles of comprehensiveness, coordination, equity, quality, nondiscrimination, transparency, participation, and accountability to prevent corruption; and ensure that the poorest and most vulnerable members of their society have effective access to healthcare services and programmes the health system offers (American Public Health Association, 2013). It should be noted that transparency and accountability have been widely accepted as key to service delivery improvements and there is no doubt that transparency and accountability lead to increase responsiveness on the part of service providers, improved access and quality of services, and consequently better health outcomes i.e. quality healthcare (Joshi, 2010).

In sharp contrast to the above information however, in a study conducted by Berlan and Shiffma (2011), it was found that healthcare providers in low-income countries such as Malawi often treat consumers poorly. Emphatically, Berlan and Shiffma (2011) state that a number of studies provide evidence that provider's accountability can be enhanced when consumers gain greater access to information pertaining to the healthcare service delivery of the country. Considering the foregoing information, it is important to say that accountability in the health sector of any country can be enhanced by ensuring that the health sector is decentralized and that there is community participation.

c) *Poor Quality of Services*

Our data also show that the quality of service clients get from the QECH is not good because mostly when they visit the hospital for treatment, they go back home without the medication they need in order for them to recover. The respondents stated that the services rendered to them by the QECH are not effective. The service receivers of the QECH noted that the QECH authorities need to improve on the quality of services they render to patients in order to make them effective. This can be seen from their response such as, *"I can say that services are not quite good here; several times we go back because there is no medicine".*[9] Another respondent particularly noted that, *"Am not satisfied with services they offer to us".*[10] Our finding also reveals that patients are of the opinion that it is only in the Emergency Department of the QECH that patients are sure of getting prompt treatment. They stated further that apart from the emergency wing of the hospital, the QECH staff in other departments do not respond to patients promptly.

---

[9] Interview
[10] Interview

The qualitative data findings are in agreement with the survey findings where the responses on the statement, "I am satisfied with the services rendered to me by this hospital", reveal that out of the 78 respondents, 36 (46.2%) strongly disagreed, and the responses on the statement, "Generally speaking, this hospital services are effective", reveal that out of the 78 respondents, 26 (33.3%) strongly disagreed, while 24 (30.8%) disagreed. These findings are not very ideal for the QECH because Kazianga et al. (2013) report that if patients are dissatisfied with the quality of care they receive, they may not adhere to the treatment regiment, or they may fail to attend follow-up visits (Kazianga et al., 2013). These findings are also supported by the results of the study conducted by Montasser et al. (2012) who report women's dissatisfaction with antenatal care and the reasons for their dissatisfaction include long waiting time, inadequate medicine supply and health workers' negative attitudes. Also, this can be the reason why Vujicic et al. (2011) report that staff productivity and the quality of care they provide have been reported to be major problems in developing countries and that such health workforce challenges are a major bottleneck to improve health systems and health service delivery in developing nations (Vujicic et al., 2011).

d) Lack of Participation from Within and from Outside

Factors which hinder quality service delivery at the QECH are that the authorities of the QECH do not allow patients the opportunity to share their views on how things are being done in the hospital. In other words, there is lack of participation from within and from outside. Most importantly, the data of this study also reveal that quality service delivery are hindered in the QECH because according to the respondents, the authorities of the Ministry of Health in Malawi do not pay adequate attention to the QECH. Our data reveal further that the present situation of the hospital is consequent to the neglect of the hospital on the part of the MOH staff. This can also be seen in the response provided by one of the service providers who explained that, *"Many problems that we experience are caused by the negligence of MOH".[11] Information dissemination procedure of the QECH is also indicated as one of the factors mitigating against quality*

---

[11] Interview

service delivery in the hospital. In this regard a midwife stated that, "There is no specific way of disseminating information to us here".[12]

Furthermore, the data analyzed show that the QECH is not in any way accountable to the patients who patronize it for treatment. In other words, the issue of accountability is conspicuously absent at the QECH according to the data obtained from the service receivers of the QECH. Additionally, the respondents went further stating that although patients who come to the QECH for treatment are sometimes given the chance to ask questions about the things they need to know, they are strictly not given any room to ask questions regarding administration procedures of the hospital. This implies that on their part they do not know how the hospital is being run by the government. Nevertheless, according to the data analyzed for this study the respondents highlighted in their responses that although the QECH is not at all accountable to them in any way, the QECH is accountable to the government of the country through the Ministry of Health and Population. This can be evidenced in a response of one of the clients, "I don't think this hospital is accountable to the people; there is no indication about that".[13] Another patient also noted that, "The hospital is not accountable to me; I don't have voice on its affairs".[14]

Furthermore, this study also reveals that junior staff (service providers) at the QECH have the opportunity to share their views during staff meetings only, but they are not fully aware of any specific decision-making wing for the QECH. Ultimately speaking, they reported that freedom of speech for them is very limited. This can be seen from the response of one of the service providers who stated that, *"Sometimes they give us chance to say what we want but mainly on issues that does not concern the administration of the hospital".[15] The qualitative data findings are in agreement with the findings garnered from the survey where the results of the respondents on all items under the dimension of accountability in the survey questionnaire yielded a total mean of 2.26 and this figure is very far below the mean, indicating that there is lack of accountability in the QECH procedures. The findings of this study are in total agreement with findings from the study conducted by Brinkerhoff (2003) who reports that although healthcare beneficiaries and*

---

12 Interview

13 Interview

14 Interview

15 Interview

patients are central to service delivery, traditionally, health systems have not accorded them much of a role in accountability. This is the true situation of the QECH in terms of accountability as revealed by the data analyzed. The aforementioned findings are issues of concern for the QECH and the MOH because according to Joshi (2010), accountability is highly indispensable in any public sector. The author contends further that accountability has been widely accepted as key to service delivery improvements and there is no doubt that transparency and accountability lead to increase responsiveness on the part of service providers, improved access and quality of services, and consequently better health outcomes i.e. quality healthcare (Joshi, 2010).

CONCLUSION

Considering the abovementioned discussions, our point of departure is that the government of Malawi through its Ministry of Health can learn more from the ways Malaysian healthcare sector operates. In Malawi, people living in the remote areas far from the medical health centers can benefit from mobile clinics if the government through the Health Ministry introduces this medical facility. Many lives can be saved from unnecessary death which in most cases occurs due to lack of quality medical facilities within a walking distance. Additionally, the Malawi healthcare sector can also learn from the Malaysian health system that the challenges faced by medical staff in the public and private hospitals can be minimized by establishing many medical training schools to increase the number of medical personnel in the country. This stance can be achieved if the government of Malawi seeks to learn from other countries such as Malaysia who was poor in the past but now can stand on its own. We further suggest the following measures may help the government of the Republic of Malawi/the Ministry of Health and more specifically at the hospital management level to improve the good governance practices:

1) The government, the Ministry of Health and the hospital management in Malawi should at all times work together in mutual synergy in order to ensure that their vision and mission i.e. the quality service delivery in the health sector are made known to the patients, both on paper and in practice in every ramification.

2) Adequate drugs and medical facilities must be made available which are indispensable to the smooth running of a hospital such as the QECH to ease the tasks of the service providers, because a healthcare system that experiences severe shortage of resources cannot perform well, meet the needs and satisfy its clients.

3) The hospital management system in Malawi should develop and encourage a participative type of management whereby patients' and subordinate staff's views can be taken into cognizance by the top management of the healthcare system because this will ensure accountability and transparency together with all other tenets of health service governance.

4) The government of Malawi should have a deliberate healthcare policy to allow and/or encourage the Ministry of Health to adopt new healthcare strategies that could be learnt from other countries such as Malaysia.

5) The government of Malawi through the Ministry of Health and Population should consider the views of the citizens pertaining to the quality of the healthcare services rendered to them and that the hospital management should be open and be accountable to the general public to ensure high-quality healthcare service delivery.

REFERENCES

Al-Hawary, S.I.S. (2012). Health care services quality at private hospitals, from patients' perspective: A comparative study between Jordan and Saudi Arabia. African *Journal of Business Management, Vol.6 (22), pp. 6516-6529.*

American Public Health Association. (2013). Strengthening Health Systems in Developing Countries: Policy Statement Database; Retrieved March 18, 2013. http://www.apha.org/advocacy/policy/policysearch/default.htm?id=1375

Awang, Z.H. (2000). Governance Innovation: The Demand side of Quality. In Good Governance: Issues and Challenges by Osman S., Et.al (2000) (1st ed) National Institute of Public Administration (INTAN) Kuala Lumpur, Malaysia.

Berlan, D., & Shiffman, J. (2011). Holding Health Providers in Developing Countries Accountable to Consumers: A Synthesis of Relevant Scholarship. Oxford University Press in association with The London School of Hygiene and Tropical Medicine, Health Policy and Planning 2012;27:271–280,USA. http://heapol.oxfordjournals.org

Brinkerhoff, D.W., & Bossert, T.J. (2008). Health Governance: Concepts, Experience, and Programming Options; USAID from the American People. Retrieved April 06 2013. http://www.healthsystems2020. org/files/1914_file_Governance_Policy_Brief_FIN_2. pdf

Browning, T. (2011). Elective attachment: Queen Elizabeth Central Hospital, Blantyre, Malawi Department of Medicine, 1 August to 9 September 2011. Retrieved December 23, 2012. http://www.medicmalawi. org/wpcontent/uploads/2012/03/TBrowning-Elective-2- 1.pdf

Changole, J., Bandawe, C., Makanani, B., Nkanaunena, K., Taulo, F., Malunga, E & Kafulafula, G. (2010). Patients' satisfaction with reproductive health services at Gogo Chatinkha Maternity Unit, Queen Elizabeth Central Hospital, Blantyre, Malawi. *Malawi Medical Journal 22(1):5-9 March 2010.*

Chigwedere, E (2009) - A Qualitative Study on Equity in Provision of ART in Malawi: A

Case study of Lilongwe District; A Dissertation Submitted in Partial Fulfillment Of the Requirements of the Master of Public Health Degree, University Of Malawi College Of Medicine, January 2009.

Chirwa, M.L. (2010). Knowledge Synthesis on Malawi Health System: Literature Review. Connecting health Research in Africa and Ireland Consortium (ChRAIC), Malawi College of Medicine. Retrieved September 22, 2012. http://www.chraic.org/wp-content/uploads/2010/09/ Malawi-Knowledge-Synthesis.pdf

Dwyer, J., & Eager, K., (2008). Options for reform of Commonwealth and State governance responsibilities for the Australian health system: A paper commissioned by the National Health and Hospitals Reform Commission.

Gauthier, B., & Reinikka, R. (2007). Methodological approaches to the study of Institutions and service delivery: A review of PETS, QSDS and CRC. Retrieved December 32, 2012. http://www.aercafrica.

org/documents/isd_workingpapers/GauthierReinikkaMethodological ApproachestotheStudyofISD.pdf

Gilson, L. (2003). Trust and the Development of Health Care as a Social Institution. Elsevier Science Ltd.Social Science & Medicine 56 (2003) 1453 1468.PERGAMON. www.elsevier.com/locate/socscimed

Idana, I, Y., S. (2006). Queen Elizabeth Central Hospital as a Centre of Excellence in ServiceProvision, Teaching, and Research: is Memorandum of Understanding the Solution: A Dissertation Submitted In Partial Fulfillment of the Requirement for the Award of the Master of Public Health Degree – College of Medicine University of Malawi.

Joshi, A. (2010). Review of Impact and Effectiveness of Transparency and Accountability Initiatives: Annex 1 Service Delivery. Institute of Development Studies. Prepared for the Transparency and Accountability Initiative Workshop October 14 – 15, 2010. Retrieved January 2, 2012. http://www.ids.ac.uk/files/dmfile/IETAAnnex1 ServicedeliveryJoshiFinal28Oct20 10.pdf

Jamaludin, N, H., Habidin, N, F., Shazali, N, A., Ali, N., Khaidir, N, A., (2013) "Exploring Sustainable Healthcare Service and Sustainable Healthcare Performance: Based on Malaysian Healthcare Industry" *Journal of Sustainable Development Studies. ISSN 2201-4268 Volume 3, Number 1, 2013, 14-26.*

Kachala, R. (2011). Environmental Health Policy and Regulation in Malawi: Report on control of Malaria in Malawi by Dr. Rabson Kachala February on 20, 2011. Retrieved October 21, 2012. http://kachala.wordpress. com/2011/02/20/environmental-health-policy-andregulation-in-malawi/

Kachiza, C.R. (2005).Analysis of Patient Care Services at Kamuzu Central Hospital: A Critical Look at the Hospital's Challenges and Opportunities in Meeting the Need: A dissertation Submitted in Partial Fulfilment of the Requirement of Master of Public Health Degree, College of Medicine University of Malawi.

Kaisi, S. A. (2013). Good Governance in the Health Sector of Malawi: A Case of Queen Elizabeth Central Hospital. A Dissertation Submitted in Fulfillment of the Requirement for the Degree of Master of Human Sciences (Political Science). Department of Political Science, International Islamic University Malaysia; June 2013.

Kazianga, H., Kouanda, E., Nikema, L., Rothenbuhler, E., Over, M., & De Walque, D. (2013). HIV services delivery and overall quality of care and satisfaction in Burkina Faso: are there privileged patients? Retrieved April 03, 2013 http://www.hkazianga.org/Ppapers/HealthFacilitiesBurkina.pdf

Market Watch, (2011). The Healthcare Sector in Malaysia

Mfutso-Bengu, J., & Muula, A.S. (2002). Is it Ethical for Health Workers to Strike? Issues from the 2001 QECH General Hospital Strike. Retrieved April 03, 2013. www.ajol.info/index.php/mmj/article/download/10766/14429

Nagata, J.M., Gatti, L.R., Barg, F.K. (2012). Social determinants of iron supplementation among women of reproductive age: a systematic review of qualitative data. Maternal and Child Nutrition, 8(1):1-18

Nyasa Times News. (2013).Malawi: of essential drug out, gluttony, garbage in, garbage out; Nyasa Times Online. Retrieved March 20, 2013. http://www.nyasatimes.com/2013/02/05/malawi-of-essential-drug-stock-outs-gluttony-and-garbage-in-garbage-out/

OXFAM International. (2008). Malawi Essential Health Services Campaign: For All Campaign: country case study. Retrieved March 20, 2013. http://www.oxfam.org/en/policy/malawi-case-study-essential-health-services

PHCFM. (2012). Determinants of patient satisfaction with outpatient health services at public and private hospitals in Addis Ababa, Ethiopia. *African Journal of primary health care and family medicine, Vol. 4, No 1.*

Schellekens, O.P., Lindner, M.E., Lang, J.M.A & Van Der Gaag, J. (2007). A new Paradigm for increased access to healthcare in Africa: A paper presented the Annual IFC / Financial Times Essay in Copenhagen; Retrieved March 12, 2013. http://www.medicalcreditfund.org/media/12005/A%20new%20paradigm%20for20increased%20access%20to%20healthcare%20in%20Africa_OS.pdf

Shazali N, S., Habidin, N, F., Ali, N., Khaidir, N, A., Jamaludin, N, H., (2013). Lean Healthcare Practice and Healthcare Performance in Malaysian Healthcare Industry. International Journal of Scientific and Research Publications, Volume 3, Issue 1, January 2013 1 ISSN 2250-3153.

Siddiqi, S., Masud, T.I., Nishtar, S., Peters, D.H., Sabri, B., Bile, K.M & Jama, M.A. (2009). Framework for assessing governance of the health system in developing Countries: Gateway to good governance. *Health Policy Vol. 90 Iss.1 (2009) 13–25.*

The World Health Organization (2009). The Performance of A National Health Workforce: How to Assess it? How to Strengthen It? An International Symposium placed under the aegis of The World Health Organization Neuchâtel, Switzerland, 14-16 October 2009; The Swiss Health Observatory, Neuchâtel, Switzerland, The Federal Office of Public Health, Bern, Switzerland, The Center for Health Workforce Studies, State University of New York, U.S.A., The Centre de Sociologie et de Démographie Médicales, Paris, France; Retrieved April 25 2013. http://www.who.int/hrh/events/symposium_workforce.pdf

United Nations Development Program. (2011). Fighting Corruption in the Health Sector Methods, Tools and Good Practices. Retrieved April 06, 2013. http://www.undp.org.tt/news/UNODC/Anticorruption%20Methods%20and%20Tools%20in%20Health%20L.

White, V.A. (2011). Malaria in Malawi Inside a Research Autopsy Study of Pediatric Cerebral Malaria. *Arch Pathol Lab Med—Vol. 135, February 2011.*

Yin, R.K. (1994). Case Study Research: Design and Methods (2nd ed.) Sage Publications, United Kingdom

Zere, E., Moeti, M., Kirigia, J., Mwase T., & Kataika, E. (2007). Equity in health and Healthcare in Malawi: analysis of trends, *BMC Public Health. 2007; 7: 78; doi: 10.1186/1471-2458-7-78.*

SOCIO-CULTURAL DETERMINANTS OF HEALTH AND WELLBEING OF YOUTH IN SUB-SAHARAN AFRICA

Adeela Rehman & Nurazzura Mohamad Diah

INTRODUCTION

Sub-Sahara Africa is a region with culturally assorted and rapidly growing population comprising of 670 million people living in 48 states and one territory. One third of its population comprises of youth aged between 10-24 years which is approximately 157 million (33%) in number with a predict able escalation to 198 million by 2015 (Barker, 2005; Population Reference Bureau, 2006). Geographically, the region is located at the south of the Sahara desert in contrast with North Africa.

This zone of Africa stretched transversely from the southern edge of the Sahara Desert at the widest portion of the continent surrounded by salt water. The Indian Ocean is located at east side of its border and the Atlantic is on the west side. The Southern peak of the continent, where the Indian Ocean and the Atlantic Ocean meet is called "Cape of Good Hope". This part of Africa continues to have low levels of literacy and life expectancy yet it has the fastest growing population in the whole world. The table below illustrates some demographical information of Africa and other major regions in the world:

Table 1 Socio-demographic characteristics of Sub-Saharan Africa and other major regions in 2001

Region	Pop. (Mil.)	Total Fertility	Life Expectancy	Population Growth (%)	Human Development Index	Per Capita GNI ($)	Adult Literacy (%)
Sub-Saharan Africa	626	5.5	47	2.4	0.468	1,830	38
North Africa and the Middle East	290	3.5	66	2.0	0.662	5,040	39
Latin America and Caribbean	523	2.6	70	1.5	0.777	7.050	11
South Asia	1,455	3.1	63	1.6	0.582	2.730	44
EAST Asia and Pacific	1,900	1.8	69	0.8	0.722	4,230	13
OECD Countries	1,141	1.7	76	0.3	9.05	23, 360	58
World	6,148	2.7	65	1.3	0.722	7,380	49

Source: UNDP (2003), United Nations (2003b) cited in Tabutin and Schoumaker (2004).

The above table shows that Sub-Saharan Africa has the most rapidly growing population in the world. The fertility rate is also higher than the rest of the world which is 5.5 children per woman as compared to women in the OECD countries which only have 1.7, the lowest in the presented data. The region also has lower life expectancy but fastest growing population.

CLIMATE AND POPULATION

Sub-Saharan Africa is the largest region of the world, around 900 million people residing in the area. It is estimated that by 2100, it will increase by 77% of the total increase in worldwide populace. Out of 54 states, 31 are predicted to have two-fold of their population by 2050. Population growth will stimulate development encounters in Africa. Changes in climate are also likely to cause scarcity in natural resources such as water and land (Population Action, 2012).

Due to its fast growing population and climate change, the region has high rates of malnutrition, infectious diseases, poverty and unemployment. Agriculture, which is largely dependent on rain, is badly affected by climate change. Due to this the region is labeled as the most susceptible part of the world due to its environmental transformation (Niang et al. 2014). The most vulnerable sector is agriculture which is the biggest source of livelihood for the largest population of the region (Serdeczny, 2016).

CULTURAL TRAITS OF SUB-SAHARAN AFRICAN SOCIETY

Sub-Saharan Africa region is diverse in languages, cultural traits, rituals and religions. More than 1,000 languages are spoken in the region (Bowden, 2007). By religion, the majority of the population in the south of Africa are Christians, while Muslims dominate in North Africa. Countries like Somalia, Sierra Leone, Tanzania, Kenya, Ethiopia, Senegal, Gambia, Guinea, Mali and Niger have Muslim population in the majority. Mauritius is the only African country having Hindu majority (Encyclopedia Britannica, 2003).

Globalization has affected all parts of Africa which is also undergoing various changes to its civilization since 1200 A.D. Due to rapid changes in climate, the Sahara Desert has limited cultural contact with Europe and the Middle East but has deep rooted traditions within their own African territories (Guisepi, 2001). Although it is the most diverse region of the world, certain common features such as race, colour, ethnicity and geographical location together represent the cultural unity of Africa. The most common feature of the society is the structure of kingship which has very strong roots in the culture and resistant to any changes (Dia, 1991).

There are a number of positive and negative stereotypes about the African continent portrayed by the society and the media too. Since the mid-1970s, the media have been portraying controversial images and reflections of the developing countries as poor and backward nations (Mahadeo, & McKinney, 2007). But with the development of the social media, the youth are trying to portray a positive image of Africa. The social media help them to change the global perceptions and overcome the negative stereotypes of Africa.

HEALTH STATUS OF YOUTH IN SUB-SAHARAN AFRICA

Youth is a very decisive phase of progression, having extensive physical strength, psycho-emotional alteration and transformation from childhood to adulthood. Therefore, the health and well-being of a youth is critical and crucial to be taken into consideration. Penetrable literature on youth health in Sub-Saharan African countries indicated how low health status negatively impact on the reproductive health of youth. This paper thus highlights general perspective of youth health and well-being concerns as well as explains the factors contributing towards increasing epidemic diseases, particularly HIV/AIDS.

The nutritional status of youth is not up to mark due to less attention given to maternal health and breastfeeding. This has resulted in malnutrition and consequently to morbidity and mortality among infants and children in Sub-Saharan Africa which leads towards poor health in teenagers too (Alles et al., 2013). Due to persistent poverty, less education and high prevalence of epidemic diseases and HIV/AIDS, these youth are underprivileged to enjoy a better life (Barker, 2005). Therefore, there are increasing health problems among youth in Africa (Blum, 2007; Kabiru et al., 2010; United Nations, 2007).

Socio-cultural gender discriminatory practices also contribute to the poor health status of youth. For instance, child and early teenage marriages are common; the majority (55%) of girls are married by the ages of 15-18 (Demographic Health Surveys, 2005-2012; UNICEF Multiple Indicator Cluster Survey, 2005-2012). Due to this, girls in this region have higher fertility rates and face more problems related to reproduction. These factors lead to higher maternal mortality rates in the region. The figure below demonstrates the regional share of mortality and HIV in global figures related to this issue.

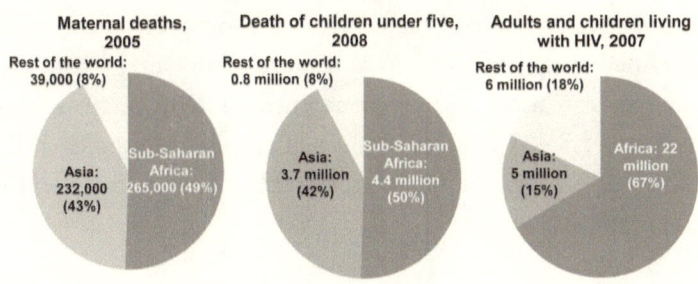

Figure 1 Regional distribution of mortality and HIV/AIDS
Source: Kinney et al. (2010)

The figure shows that more than 50% of the global burden of maternal mortality, death of children (< 5 years) and adults living with HIV are mostly contributed by Sub-Saharan Africa populace.

PREVALENCE OF HIV/AIDS

HIV/AIDS is the foremost health concern worldwide particularly in Sub-Saharan Africa which is the most affected region with numbers affected on the rise. Sub-Saharan Africa is the ruthlessly aggraveted by HIV/AIDS (Lau & Muula, 2004). According to WHO's (2016) estimation, 55% of the Sub-Saharan Africa's HIV infected population comprise of women, children and the elderly. The figures in the table below illustrate the percentage of affected population in the region.

Table 2 HIV/AIDS Prevalence in Sub-Saharan Population

Year 2015	Number of people living with HIV	People newly infected with HIV	AIDS Deaths
Total	36.7 million	2.1 million	1.1 million
Adults	34.9 million	1.9 million	1.0 million
Women (15+)	17.8 million	-	-
Children (<15 years)	1.8 million	150 000	110 000

Source: WHO-HIV Department (2016)

The above table demonstrates that adults are infected with HIV among the total population living with HIV/AIDS. Children less than 15 years of age have also contracted HIV. It shows very alarming figures which are increasing year by year and more adults are getting infected. As far as gender differences are concerned, in 2009 it was estimated 1.4% males and 3.4% females in the region are living with HIV. The following figures show the prevalence of HIV among male and female youth population:

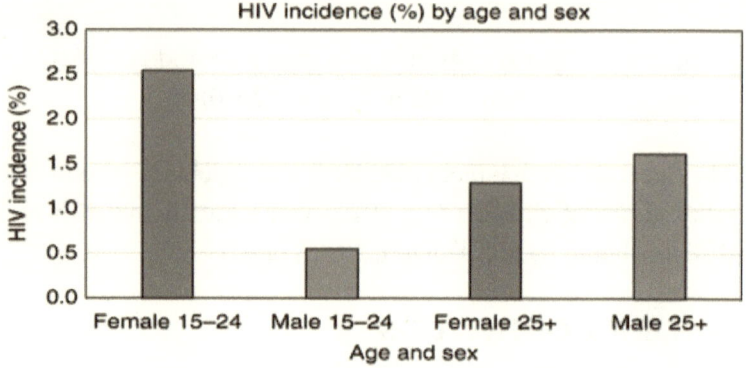

Figure 2 Comparison between HIV, gender and age

Formerly, countries such as Ethiopia, Kenya, Tanzania and Zambia have accomplished a considerable decrease of more than 25% HIV prevalence among young people. More females have been infected than males. In addition, HIV prevalence is higher in the 20-24 year-old age group (both male and female) compared to the 15-19 year-old age group, suggesting that more efforts are needed to strengthen HIV prevention for young adults, their partners and their children (Babalola, 2012). The ratio of HIV prevalence is also different among different countries of Sub-Saharan Africa as shown in figure below:

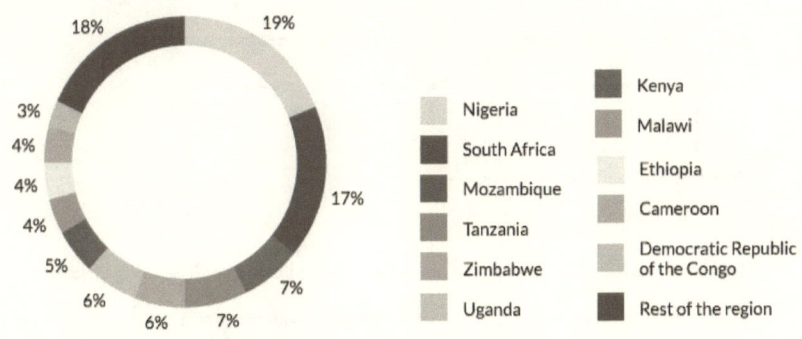

AIDS-related deaths in Sub-Saharan Africa, 2013

Figure 3 AIDS-related deaths in Sub-Saharan Countries
Source: UNAIDS: The Gap Report (2014)

The table illustrates that Nigeria has the highest HIV related deaths, followed by South Africa and while the lowest number is in the Democratic Republic of the Congo. Cameroon, Ethiopia, Malawi, Kenya, Uganda, Zimbabwe, Tanzania and Mozambique have 4-7% of deaths due to AIDS. The rest of the region of the Sub-Saharan Africa share 18% of HIV related deaths in the region.

CAUSES OF HIV AND MODE OF TRANSFORMATION

The prominent reasons for alarming figures of HIV and AIDS in this region are the socio-cultural determinants and taboos particularly related to the reproductive health and sexual activities, increasing men's and women's vulnerability to this disease. The taboos related to seeking sexual knowledge have been impeding the youth from being aware of their reproductive health system and HIV (Global Report, 2012). Gender based violence has also increased this burden of HIV such as sexual harassment, rape, marital rape, and sexual assault etc. Sexual violence can result in 'direct transmission' of HIV which can be the result of forced or forcible sexual intercourse with an HIV infected partner (Wight et al., 2006). The next diagram shows the interrelated problems among children and families affected by HIV/AIDS.

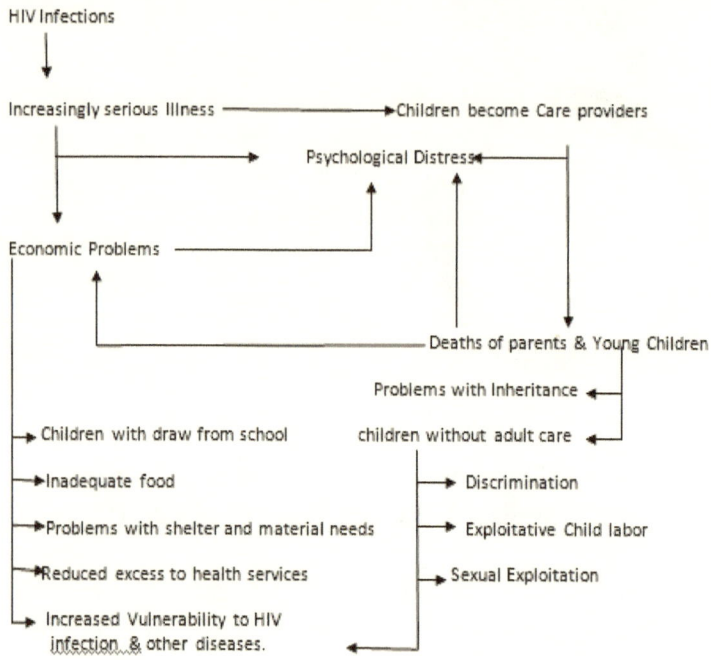

Diagram 1 Factors contributing to HIV/AIDS
Source: Fostera and Williamson (2000)

Besides various social-cultural problems of having HIV/AIDS, sexual activities and other related risk factors such as multiple partners, IDU, etc. also contribute to its increase as shown in the figure below.

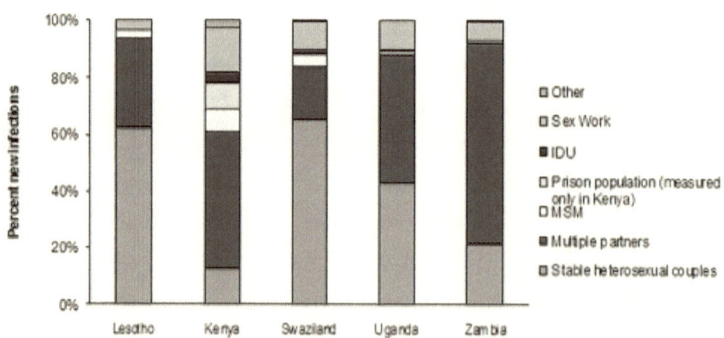

Figure 4. Proportion of new HIV infections in Africa
Source: UNAID (2010)

Numerous research (Shelton et al., 2005; Holmqvist, 2009; Hunter, 2007; Rodrigo & Rajapakse, 2010) indicate that people belonging to poor socio-economic class have positive association with HIV/AIDS. Poverty increases the vulnerability of both men and women to have contemporaneous heterosexual relationships. However, the prevalence of HIV is more in urban areas due to its over population and people living in small houses. The next figure shows the number of urban and rural population who have been infected by HIV.

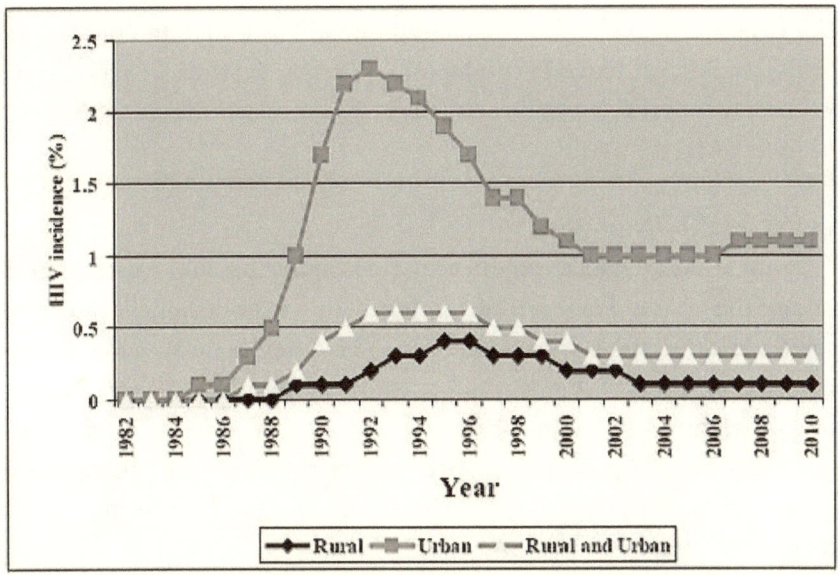

Figure 5 Rural-Urban statistics on HIV Prevalence
Source: WHO, Regional Office Africa (2016)

ACCESSIBILITY TO HEALTH SERVICES

Besides all these factors, young people in Africa are also faced with considerable impediments in accessing health services (Tylee et al., 2007). WHO (2010) indicates that most of Sub-Saharan African countries have a shortage of youth friendly health services and insufficient policies to address their health needs. Several studies (Stefan, 2008; Biddlecom, 2007) mentioned that reproductive health service utilization is not fulfilling the needs of youth. Lack of education, unemployment and poverty in Sub-Saharan Africa, add towards deteriorating the reproductive health of youth. The health facilities are not youth friendly and lack potential to provide the services according to the needs of growing adults (Tylee et al., 2007). The health policies and programmes are inadequate to address the youth's health concerns (WHO, 2010). Even the health services lack specialized care by the professionals who lack up-to-date knowledge to deal with the health problems of the youth (Stefan, 2008).

To overcome the problems of increasing HIV/AIDS the National Strategic Plan (NSP) of South Africa had initiated antiretroviral treatment (ART) between 2007-2011. The programme still continues and the current NSP from 2012-2016 has been adopted and promoted the UNAIDS vision of "Zero new HIV Infections and Zero AIDS related death" (SANAC, 2011; UNAIDS, 2011).

CONCLUSION

Sub-Saharan Africa experiences poor nutrition and health status among the youth. There is need to invest in the health of the youth to make a healthy change into adulthood. The government should focus its attention on the development of youth by establishing effective policies and programmes to promote healthy living. The state must establish collaboration and partnership with donors to generate more funds to promote research activities in determining the health problems of the youth in the region.

Youth in Sub-Saharan Africa are facing numerous health challenges which are distressing on the overall development of the region. The factors regarding the situation and research evidence are necessary to understand the matters that aggravate the health concerns of youth in the region. The existing literature on health and well-being of youth in Sub-Saharan Africa is inadequate and concentrate mainly on HIV/AIDS problems. The general well-being of youth in terms of their nutritional status, health living standards and common health complications need to be addressed in forthcoming studies.

REFERENCES

Alles M, Eussen S, Ake-Tano O, Diouf S, Tanya A, Lakati A, Oduwole A, Mauras C. (2013). Situational analysis and expert evaluation of the nutrition and health status of infants and young children in five countries in sub-Saharan Africa. *Food Nutrition Bulletin*, 34(3), 287-98.

Ashford L. S. (2007). Africa's youthful population: Risk or opportunity. Washington, DC: Population Reference Bureau.

Babalola, S., David, A., & Brigitte, Q. R. (2002). The correlates of safe sex practices among Rwandan youth: a positive deviance approach. *African Journal of AIDS Research*, 1, 11-21.

Barker, D. & Ricardo C. (2005).Young Men and the Construction of Masculinity in Sub-Saharan Africa. Social Development Papers No. 26. Washington: The World Bank.

Biddlecom, A. E, Munthali, A., Singh, S., Woog, V. (2007). Adolescents' views of and preferences for sexual and reproductive health services in Burkina Faso, Ghana, Malawi and Uganda. *African Journal of Reproductive Health*, 11(3), 99-100.

Blum, R. W. (2007). Youth in sub-Saharan Africa. *Journal of Adolescents Health*, 41, 230-238.

Blum, R. W., Bastosm, F. I., & Kabiru, C. W. (2012).Adolescent health in the 21st century. *The Lancet,* 379 (9826), 1567–1568

Bowden, Rob (2007). *Africa South of the Sahara*. Coughlan Publishing

Caroline, W. K., Chimarakoe, O. L., & Dounatien, B. (2013). The health and wellbeing of young people in sub-Saharan Africa: an under-researched area? *BMC International Health Human Rights*, 13, 11.

Dia, M. (1991). Development and cultural values in sub-Saharan Africa. *Finance and Development, 28*(4), 10.

Encyclopedia Britannica. Britannica Book of the Year 2003. (2003)

Foster, G., & Williamson, J. (2000). A review of current literature on the impact of HIV/AIDS on children in sub-Saharan Africa.

Global (2012).Joint United Nations Programme on HIV/AIDS (UNAIDS) Global Report on HIV/AIDS.

Guisepi, R. A. (2001). Africa, Emerging Civilizations In Sub-Sahara Africa Various Authors. History World International publication

Holmqvist G. (2009) HIV and income inequality, IPC working paper 54. International Policy Centre for Inclusive Growth: Brasilia; 2009.

Hunter, M. 2007. The changing political economy of sex in South Africa: The significance of unemployment and inequalities to the scale of the AIDS pandemic, Social Science & Medicine 64(3):689-700

June 2012, Population Action International and the African Institute for Development Policy, Population, Climate Change, and Sustainable Development in Africa. wwww.populationaction.org

Kabiru C. W, Undie C, Ezeh A. C (2010). In Routledge handbook of global public health. Parker R, Sommer M, editor. London: Routledge; 2010. A generation at risk: Prioritizing child and youth health; pp. 182–190.

Kinney MV, Kerber KJ, Black RE, Cohen B, Nkrumah F, Coovadia H, Nampala PM, Lawn JE, Science in Action: Saving the lives of Africa's Mothers, Newborns, and Children working group

Axelson H, Bergh AM, Chopra M, Diab R, Friberg I, Odubanjo O, Walker N, Weissman E-PLoS Med. (2010)

Lau, C., & Muula, A. S. (2004). HIV/AIDS in Sub-Saharan Africa.

Mahadeo, M & McKinney, J (2007) 'Media representations of Africa: Still the same old story?', Policy & Practice: A Development Education Review, Vol. 4, Spring, pp. 14-20.

Niang I, Ruppel OC, Abdrabo MA, Essel A, Lennard C, Padgham J, Urquhart P (2014) Africa. In: Climate change 2014: impacts, adaptation and vulnerability. Contribution of Working Group II to the Fifth Assessment Report of the Intergovernmental Panel on Climate Change. Cambridge University Press, Cambridge

Population Reference Bureau (2006).World's Youth 2006 Data Sheet. Washington DC:

Rodrigo, C. and S. Rajapakse. 2010. HIV, poverty and women, International Health 2(1):9- 16.

Serdeczny, O., Adams, S., Baarsch, F., Coumou, D., Robinson, A., Hare, W. & Reinhardt, J. Climate change impacts in Sub-Saharan Africa: from physical changes to their social repercussions. *Regional Environmental Change*, 1-16.

Shelton, J.D., M.M. Cassell, and J. Adetunji (2005). Is poverty or wealth at the root of HIV? The Lancet, 366(9491):1057-1058

South African National AIDS Council (SANAC) (2011) 'National Strategic Plan on HIV, STIs and TB 2012-2016'. *South Africa Medical Journal*, 98(3), 184-187.

Stefan C. (2008). Treating adolescents in South Africa: time for adolescent medicine units?

Sub-Saharan Africa's mothers, newborns, and children: where and why do they die? *South Africa Medical Journal*. 98(3):184–187.

Tabutin, D & Schoumaker, B (2004). The Demography of Sub-Saharan Africa from the 1950s to the 2000s. A Survey of Changes and a Statistical Assessment. *Population* (Vol. 59) Pages 521 – 622

Tylee A, Haller D. M., Graham, T., Churchill, R., & Sanci, L.A (2007). Youth-friendly primary-care services: how are we doing and what more needs to be done? *Lancet*, 369 (9572), 1565-1573.

UNAIDS (2011, 20 December) 'South Africa launches its new National Strategic Plan on HIV, STIs and TB, 2012–2016'

UNAIDS. Regional Support Team for Eastern and Southern Africa – modes of transmission.http://www.unaidsrstesa.org/hiv-prevention-modes-of-transmission Accessed March 8, 2010.

United Nations (2007). The World Youth Report 2007: Young People's Transition to Adulthood: Progress and Challenges. New York: United Nations.

World Health Organization (2010).*Child and Adolescent Health Annual Report,* Brazzaville, Republic of Congo: WHO.

World Health Organization (Regional Office for Africa) Child and Adolescent Health Annual Report, 1 January – 31 December 2010. Brazzaville, Republic of Congo: WHO/AFRO; 2010.